"Dr. Beverly J. Gaard shares through lively experiences and invaluable techniques. The stories in this book will awaken anyone to their potential. The book is easy to read and the principles show how to connect with Universal Laws."

—Dr. Roger A. Weiss,
Psychologist
Kailua-Kona, Hawaii

"The teachings explained in this book have changed my life in the most profound ways. Everyone can learn from this material to manifest miracles in their lives. I have done it, and I am forever grateful to Dr. Gaard for bringing forth this knowledge."

—Stepfanie Kramer
Actress, singer
Los Angeles, California

"The National Academy of Metaphysics and Chirothesia has changed my life and given me the tools to live in harmony, good health, and an abundant life and career. Finding my true love and living these principles daily in my marriage has made our love stronger each day."

—Arlene Matza Jackson
Alethea Music
Songwriter, producer
Los Angeles, California

"Beverly Gaard has helped thousands of students better their lives in every way—spiritually, mentally, and physically. I was one of them. Beverly helped me transform my life."

—Richard Wagner,
R. Zach Jewelers
Beverly Hills, California

"Dr. Beverly J. Gaard has awakened in me the formerly unknown dynamic force available to us all. She guided me to an abundant life filled with joy and gratitude."

—Frances Scully Jr.
Chairmen, Financial Guaranty Insurance Brokers, Inc.
Pasadena, California

"I have immeasurable gratitude for all the positive changes in my life due to the teaching as delivered by Dr. Gaard. Every area of my life has changed for the better since I studied and have used the Universal Laws for my meditation each day."

—Valli Aman
Intuitive Dog Whisperer
Oh My Dog
Los Angeles, California

I was there

The Law of Miracles in Action

Dr. Beverly J. Gaard

BALBOA.
PRESS
A DIVISION OF HAY HOUSE

Balboa Press books may be ordered through booksellers or by contacting:

Balboa Press
A Division of Hay House
1663 Liberty Drive
Bloomington, IN 47403
www.balboapress.com
1 (877) 407-4847

Because of the dynamic nature of the Internet, any web addresses or
links contained in this book may have changed since publication and
may no longer be valid. The views expressed in this work are solely those
of the author and do not necessarily reflect the views of the publisher,
and the publisher hereby disclaims any responsibility for them.

The author of this book does not dispense medical advice or prescribe the use
of any technique as a form of treatment for physical, emotional, or medical
problems without the advice of a physician, either directly or indirectly. The
intent of the author is only to offer information of a general nature to help
you in your quest for emotional and spiritual well-being. In the event you use
any of the information in this book for yourself, which is your constitutional
right, the author and the publisher assume no responsibility for your actions.

Any people depicted in stock imagery provided by Thinkstock are models,
and such images are being used for illustrative purposes only.
Certain stock imagery © Thinkstock.

Printed in the United States of America.

ISBN: 978-1-4525-9292-3 (sc)
ISBN: 978-1-4525-9294-7 (hc)
ISBN: 978-1-4525-9293-0 (e)
Library of Congress Control Number: 2014903216

Balboa Press rev. date: 04/15/2014

To my beloved Master teacher, Dr. DJ Bussell;
without him, I would never have made it.

CONTENTS

ACKNOWLEDGMENTS

My sincerest gratitude to Mary Marlow, who generously gave editing time for more than a year.

My love and heartfelt gratitude to Eve Ewing and Grace Bonnell for sharing their knowledge about Dr. Bussell.

I am so grateful for the thousands of students who have learned and passed on the teaching of the Universal Laws, and especially for the Inner Circle: Arlene, Jon, Bill, Richard, Valli, Stepfanie, Chelsea, Judith, Ozebia, Tracy, Diane, Cheryl, Lyle, and Teri.

Thank you Charlie and Maria, my editors to the end.

I want to thank my daughter, Dr. Greta Gaard, and my late husband, Robert Gaard; without them, I would never have had the opportunity to practice what I learned.

Deepest gratitude to Dr. George E. Patterson for his medical explanation of what we call the "Kingdom of God"

Lastly, my husband of twenty-five years, Charles, my proofreader, without whom I would have starved.

INTRODUCTION

Can you remember anything before you were born? Think for a moment! How far back can you remember? How far back does your consciousness go? Where were you just before you came into this world? It's not hard to imagine if you take the time to be still.

I did take the time to be still, and I remember. That scene has remained with me all my life. It felt like there was no beginning or end. I was just consciousness. I was conscious of being an individual consciousness. Does that make sense?

I remember it was very dark, and I was in blackness, but I knew I wasn't alone. There was a very large Presence, close and watching over me. I didn't feel like a baby or a human being. I felt as if I was about to embark on a new adventure. I saw a light, and then I was born. I will never forget this event. It's as much a part of me as my body is.

As a growing child, I wanted to find this Presence. I searched many religions: Presbyterian, Episcopalian, Hinduism, Catholicism, and Judaism.

As I grew older, I found myself dissatisfied being a receptionist, hostess, model, and actress. I turned down many opportunities to be successful instead looking for something else that was more important to me, but I didn't know where to find it.

At the age of twenty-seven, I married. Despite being happy, it wasn't the answer I had been searching for. However, it was the right move because, along with my husband, I met Carroll Righter, the famous Hollywood astrologer of the 1950s. It must have been my destiny because Mr. Righter introduced me to the man who changed—no *saved*—my life. I don't even want to think of what my life would have been without finding him.

I knew he was the one I was looking for the moment I sat down in a remodeled front room of an old house in Hollywood, which had been converted into a church. I knew it the moment he walked into the room, stepped on the platform, and began to speak. I knew it when he began to take us through what is known as the Harmony Exercise. I felt as if I had been through the exercise many times before because it felt so familiar to me. The joy and relief were overwhelming.

This is a story of my encounter with a man whose life was dedicated to Westernizing the Eastern teaching and saving as many lives as he could by his example. He taught the Universal Laws of God and how to live these laws in our daily lives: to be healthy in mind and body, to think and transform negative situations into positive working truths, to live in abundance of enough and to spare, to heal and be healed, to be protected wherever we are, to know and feel the peace that "passeth all understanding," and to be aware of our pervasive connection to the power and presence that is God.

Through my personal experience, you will learn the truth that you have been seeking as I guide you into a better understanding of life and how to live it in a new way.

CHAPTER 1

The Meeting

"Get up, you lazy lowlife. I'm picking you up at 10:30 this morning. We're going to church," Carroll Righter said in a very definite tone.

Well, that was unexpected, to say the least. I hung up the phone and made sure my husband, Robert Gaard, and I were ready by 10:30. Carroll was not the type of man you kept waiting.

In the 1950s, Carroll Righter was known as the world's greatest astrologer. He had a worldwide syndicated column in 306 newspapers each week, reaching thirty million homes. He had many famous clients, such as Robert Mitchum, Jayne Mansfield, Arlene Dahl, Peter Lawford, Sylvia Kaye, Polly Bergen—even Mr. and Mrs. Ronald Reagan were among his admirers. Carroll was also featured on the cover of *Time Magazine* on March 21, 1969, with a story on astrology. In addition to his greatness and fame, Carroll was known as an eccentric.

Carroll Righter, known as the world's greatest astrologer.

I was there

I first met Carroll at the Hollywood Gourmet Restaurant in Hollywood, California, which was managed by my husband. I was a hostess. The renowned ventriloquist Edgar Bergen, father of actress Candace Bergen, owned the Hollywood Gourmet, and Carroll was a regular customer. You couldn't miss him. He was a tall, thin man with a raucous laugh and a great sense of humor. When he sat down at the table, he upset the saltshakers, threw the forks and spoons in the air, untied the waitresses' sashes, and flipped the waiters' ties. This was all in fun, however, since his strict Philadelphia upbringing never gave him a chance to be a child. He often said he was getting even.

Every month, Carroll hosted a birthday party at his home on Franklin Avenue in Hollywood for the people in that month's astrological sign. The animal representing the sign always graced the front lawn. In August, representing the sign of Leo, a real live lion would lie on the grass with a watchful guard attending. In December, an elephant occupied the lawn, and the "Zodiac Parade" continued throughout the year. It certainly attracted attention, and attracting attention was one of Carroll's many gifts.

At one of his many parties, a young aspiring starlet and her escort came in, and Carroll proceeded to untie the bow on the front of her dress. Much to everyone's surprise, the starlet's dress fell to the floor, and she was stark naked. Carroll was visibly shaken, agitated, and ill at ease. He immediately whisked the starlet and her escort out of the house and sent them home.

One Sunday in the spring of 1952, Robert and I, along with several famous actors and successful professionals, were invited for breakfast at Carroll's home. Many aspiring actors wanted to be seen at one of Carroll Righter's parties. Although I was an actress and model, I honestly felt that Robert could benefit more from our association with Carroll and possibly help bring more business to the restaurant.

Carroll's home was always open to people, and I felt extremely privileged to be a guest in his home. Carroll, however, would invite people in and suddenly disappear. There was an air of mystery about him because no one knew when or if he would return, and this particular Sunday morning was no exception.

As I looked around, I realized our host was conspicuously absent, evidently to no one's surprise. I inquired of the beautiful red-haired actress, Arlene Dahl, whom I adored, as to Carroll's whereabouts.

"Oh, he'll be here soon. I think he's in church," she said.

"In church! That's a surprise," I said. It was rare to see famous people in church. No doubt they didn't want to be recognized, or perhaps they thought they didn't need any religion.

"What church?" I asked.

"I don't know. He doesn't talk much about it, and no one seems to know," she said sweetly, as if this feature was yet another aspect of Carroll's eccentricity.

Carroll Righter wasn't always a famous astrologer to the stars. He was an attorney in Philadelphia with little interest in astrology. Due to an old back injury, which became life threatening, he consulted with Evangeline Adams, a famous author, astrologer, and friend of his family, who checked the aspects in his astrological chart. Evangeline told him if he moved southwest, he would regain his health. While still in his thirties, Carroll packed his car, left Philadelphia, and moved to the West Coast. After a short period of time in the California sun, fresh air, and restful Pacific Ocean, his health significantly improved.

Even though he had tried to disprove it, Carroll became convinced there was sufficient help and direction to be found in astrology. Since he had been helped through this science, he was assured he could help others with their problems too, and soon the opportunity was presented.

After reading the astrological chart of the glamorous movie star Marlene Dietrich, Carroll warned her to avoid working on the set at the studio. Dietrich, however, did not heed his advice and broke her ankle on the set. The word of this spread and brought Carroll to the attention of many famous politicians, dignitaries, and other movie stars, such as Joan Fontaine, Grace Kelly, Rhonda Fleming, and Robert Mitchum, who at one time worked as his ghostwriter.

So, as his guests and I waited patiently for Carroll to return, I grew more and more interested in learning of his religion and philosophy since he was a loving, happy, abundant, peaceful, and successful person. I had been a spiritual seeker since my childhood, and I studied many religions in the hopes of finding my own spiritual path.

In my search to find a teacher as a child, I even trudged in the snow in Omaha all by myself to attend Sunday school at the Presbyterian church. As a family, we had stopped attending the Sunday service because Daddy snored. Later, Mother joined the choir, and then nobody could sleep!

By the time I was seven, I was turned off to church. This happened when the minister couldn't answer my question, "What was before the beginning?"

"We have to have faith," is all he said, but that was not enough for me. I could still remember the time before I was born. I'm grateful for the clear memory I had of my life before birth. I will never forget the feeling I had of the vastness of the universe, the oneness, the wholeness, the all-encompassing love of the Presence. I felt like a soul without a body somewhere in space, a child of a protective, loving parent, waiting to be born. I had no fear, but I recall being anxious when I asked the Creator, the all-knowing God, "When will I see light?"

"Soon," was the only comforting, soft, loving answer I received. I asked this in thought, and the answer returned in thought. This communication was in consciousness, and I wanted it to take place sooner, but I had to wait. Then, shortly, I was born and came into this world.

Through the years, I had been a Presbyterian and an Episcopalian. I had converted to Judaism, studied Catholicism, and then comparative religions. I was determined to know what path Carroll Righter was following, even though his spiritual actions appeared to be a well-kept secret by everyone who knew him.

Upon Carroll's gregarious entrance back to his home, I was finally able to corner him and ask about the church he attended. I wanted to know everything. What was the religion? Where was the church located? What was the philosophy? I asked very respectfully.

He was, of course, evasive and changed the subject, but I pursued with determination. However, when he continued not to respond, I regretfully dropped the subject. I didn't want to irritate him. Maybe I would try another time. There would be other Sundays, and so I waited.

A week after my intense questioning, Sunday morning at exactly 8:00, Carroll called and greeted me with his favorite expression: "Get up, you lazy lowlife. I'm picking you up at 10:30 this morning. We're going to church."

I was excited to think I would now know the secret Carroll had been hiding. Robert and I rushed to get ready before Carroll arrived. He drove up exactly at 10:30 a.m. I asked where we were going, but his only response was, "Wait and see." He wanted to keep me in suspense, and it worked. I kept watching the streets to see if I could figure out where we were headed. He turned north on Normandie and Hollywood Boulevard and drove into a small parking lot in back of what looked like a large old house with an extended front room that almost reached the sidewalk. I followed, hesitantly, through the double doors in the front entrance and suddenly found myself in a church. The church was simple, plain, and quiet. The only plaque on the wall read: *Be Happy.*

Oh great, I thought. I was far from happy at the time and didn't need a sign to remind me of just how unhappy I was. Robert and I had been going through some difficulties and knew we had to find a way to improve our relationship or our marriage wasn't going to last. Robert had been in the service in World War II, and it left quite a mark on his personality. He was full of suppressed anger, fear, and insecurity.

When we first met in Colorado Springs, Colorado, I was twenty-seven, an actress under contract to the Alexander Commercial Film Company. Robert was twenty-eight and in the Army Special Service Department at Camp Carson.

He startled me when he said, "You are the 'Beverly' I have been looking for all my life." I later found out he had even named his baby sister "Beverly" before she was born, thinking she would be the one he wanted in his life. Robert was a fascinating guy with black curly hair, brown eyes, and a great sense of humor, which was immensely entertaining. He was short in stature, evenly tempered, but withdrawn. Robert never shared his inner feelings about anything, which made it impossible for me to communicate with him. I hoped that we could work it out if we had the right counseling,.

Inspiration came when I looked at the gold letters over the header at the church: "Ye shall know the Truth and the Truth shall Make you Free, John 8:32."

The sea mist color on the walls was peaceful, and I soon felt very comfortable sitting in that calming room. The church held almost one hundred people, and as I looked around, I noticed most of them appeared to be couples who were older than Robert and me. This somehow made me hopeful that we had found the right place because our marriage wasn't going to last much longer without new direction. I really felt like we were hanging on by a thread.

The pianist played the opening hymn, and as we stood to sing, the minister, dressed in a black robe, walked onto the platform. He had thinning gray hair, and his cherubic, smiling face made him appear almost ageless. His eyes were the softest, most loving hazel eyes I had ever seen. When he began to speak, I was mesmerized. I had tears in my eyes. My inner feelings told me he was more than a minister—and that my search for a mentor was over. An aura of peace radiated from him and permeated the entire congregation. Even the tone of his voice was healing. I'm sure everyone thought so because the church was so still while he spoke.

When the service ended, the three of us walked to the front door, and Carroll introduced us to the minister. His name was Dr. Bussell. He smiled, took my hand, and held it for a moment, connecting with me on a level I had never felt before. He said, "If you want action, you'll find it here."

Chills shot up my spine. I was surprised to hear his comment. How did he know "action" was exactly what I was looking for? Following the introduction, Robert, Carroll, and I walked away in total silence.

As we were walking out to the car, Carroll stopped abruptly and said, "Wait! I have to ask Doctor something."

Robert and I waited a few minutes in the parking lot, and Carroll came back wearing a broad smile. "Just as I thought!" he said with satisfaction.

I didn't understand what he was talking about and asked, "What do you mean?"

"I asked Doctor if you were both ready," he replied.

Ready for what, I wondered … *to be a part of his congregation? Or, perhaps something else?* "Well, what did he say?" I asked, impatiently awaiting his answer.

As we drove out of the parking lot, Carroll's happy voice put us in a hopeful mood when he told us what Dr. Bussell had said: *Yes, I've been waiting for them.*

But how could he be waiting for us? He didn't even know us … or did he? Suddenly, I knew I didn't have to seek any further … I was home!

Portrait of Dr. Bussell.

CHAPTER 2

Who Is Dr. Bussell?

Could Dr. DJ Bussell be the teacher I had been seeking all my life? It is said, "When the student is ready, the teacher appears." In other words, if it is your destiny, and you are ready, you will find your teacher.

For as long as I could remember, my greatest desire had been to find someone who could take the place of the Voice of Truth I heard before I was born. I knew it was Truth because it gave me such peace and joy.

I had searched to find someone who could be my inspiration, create miracles, teach me how to love unconditionally, heal me, and guide me through life. Could Dr. Bussell possibly be my teacher of destiny? I was almost afraid to believe that he was the one I was seeking. I was determined to find out more about this mysterious man, who quietly healed so many people who flocked from all over the world to consult him. Since I didn't want to be disappointed or hasty in my decision, I encouraged Robert to attend Dr. Bussell's classes with me.

Dr. Bussell started by teaching us meditation, explaining the difference between Occidental and Eastern teaching. For instance, there is a difference in posture. Easterners sit cross-legged with their hands palms-up, and Westerners sit in chairs with their hands palms-down in their laps. With hands palms-up, you are receptive to anything, even thoughts that are negative or harmful; with hands palms-down, you are closed off to any negativity. That is why we meditate with hands palms-down. In fact, Dr. Bussell said in a lighthearted manner, "If you meditate with hands palms-up, I will not be responsible for what happens."

Dr. Bussell Westernized the Eastern teachings by simplifying the explanation of the Universal Laws and how to apply and live them in your daily life. The Universal Laws, also referred to as Spiritual Laws or Laws Of Nature, are the unwavering and unchanging principles that govern every aspect of the universe and are the means by which our world and the entire cosmos continue to exist, thrive, and expand.

The Universal Laws are founded on the understanding that everything in the universe is energy. Our thoughts, feelings, words, and actions are all forms of energy. What we think, feel, say, and do in each moment comes back to us and creates our realities. Because of this, we have the power to control our thoughts and emotions and create a world of peace, harmony, and abundance.

Dr. Bussell was a student of world religions and deciphered many ancient languages, including Greek and Latin. He said, "When you know the Universal Law, which is not a religion, it doesn't matter whether you are Catholic, Jewish, Christian, or Buddhist, it makes you a better whatever you are."

The lessons Dr. Bussell gave us were stepping-stones to self-realization, knowledge, spiritual development, and cosmic attunement. Most of all, he helped us understand how to apply the Universal Laws in everyday life, in order to discover the God-given power within, transforming negative situations into positive ones so that we may live in health, harmony, abundance, peace, and love, which is our inheritance.

As time passed, I realized Dr. Bussell was more than the minister's robe he wore. He had the power to foresee events. He was clairvoyant; he knew where you were and *how* you were. He knew if you were in trouble and needed help. When Dr. Bussell looked at you, he knew your past, present, and future. He healed blindness, every form of disease, protected you from illness or accident, repaired marriages, answered all your questions, and transformed thousands of lives.

I talked to many people who were healed through Dr. Bussell, in mind and body. He had the ability to look through your body and see how your organs functioned—pinpointing where there was a problem—and knew what to do about it, much like Edgar Cayce, who was well known as the Sleeping Prophet in the 1920s. Mr. Cayce was a psychic and healer, who would put himself in a trance and perform readings, answering questions for anyone with a problem. Dr. Bussell could diagnose and heal the same as Edgar Cayce without putting himself in a trance.

To my surprise, I learned that Dr. Bussell had actually healed himself years earlier. In 1905, Dr. Bussell had a horse-riding accident, which left him walking with great difficulty and pain for sixteen years. His focused, conscious thought was knowing, without a shadow of a doubt, the perfection of what he was visualizing. He imagined a light as a cord running through his spine, and with every small step he took, he was able to rewire his severed spinal cord with Light.

In a lecture Dr. Bussell gave on September 30, 1951, he said, "I was unable to walk even one step; the process of healing came, and today I recognize my freedom from that condition. While I do not walk, possibly, as well as some, I think the average person does not realize that there is anything wrong."

Dr. Beverly J. Gaard

He elaborated more on his condition in his lesson on "living health" in July 26, 1959.

> "The last time I learned to walk, it took a long time. I do not think it was nearly so hard the first time; I do not remember it. But I was a man and had not walked for many, many years; and then, when I had to begin to learn to walk, it took time and was very discouraging. I would see other persons get up from a chair and start to walk across the room. I couldn't do it. And to this day I cannot get up out of a chair and start to walk without thinking, 'Right, left, right', as long as I am on my feet. So we do have a struggle overcoming these conditions—some with one thing, some with another. You do not change overnight."

Dr. Bussell was a renowned world teacher, healer, traveler, attorney, and translator of Aramaic, Hebrew, and Sanskrit, and he spent over sixty years studying and translating the ancient records of the Essenes. The Jewish sect, the Essenes, authored the sacred writings of the Dead Sea Scrolls, whose ancient secrets remained hidden in the Judean desert for nearly two thousand years.

Known as the Essenes in Palestine and Syria, they were also called the Stoics in North Africa, the Therapeuti of Greece, and the Gnostics in Persia and Chaldea. They were disciplined, charitable, kind, and quiet. They practiced angelology and lived the law of harmony, health, abundance, and right action. They were the most highly evolved people on the face of the earth.

Many religions have embraced the Essene teachings since this was the original Law of God. In Sumatra, tiles and stones with markings of the Essenes, judged to be at least ten thousand years old, have been found. There is historical reference of the

Essenes as a local group covering a period of about 363 years, from 200 BC to AD 163.

It is believed Jesus followed the Essene teachings since he adhered to their codes, laws, and principles, and Mary and Joseph were also Essenes.

The Dead Sea Scrolls were discovered in 1947 in the rocky caves of the Wadi Qumran by Bedouin shepherds. The teachings in these scrolls gave new insight into the nature of the Bible and glimpses into the birth of Christianity and modern Judaism.

Two thousand years ago, before the birth of Jesus the Christ, the teachings of the Essenes were kept secret because the lessons could be mistakenly misunderstood and used destructively rather than constructively. They were protected from those who might not be sincere in their quests. In order to prevent mistakes in accepting those who were not pure in heart, there was a three-year waiting period to join the Ancient Order of the Essenes, during which one was placed on probation and closely observed. Their teachings were only given to the dedicated, disciplined, loyal, and sincere students.

According to Dr. Bussell and his research, the Essenes laid the foundation for a Messiah, whom they believed to be Jesus the Christ.

From his years of study of the Essenes, Dr. Bussell wrote an eight-course study of the Universal Laws in 1922. The course of the National Academy of Metaphysics contained the Law of God and the secret teachings of the Essenes.

Metaphysics is the study of that which is beyond the physical. *Meta* means beyond, and *physics* refers to the physical. Dr. Bussell further explained the meaning of metaphysics: *The science of being; man's relationship to his creator.*

Because of my desire to learn more ancient truth, Robert and I joined the National Academy of Metaphysics, and we were surprised at the large cross-section of people who surrounded Dr. Bussell. I met bank presidents, gardeners, actors, salesmen, business owners, and attorneys. These same people attended every meeting, and if one moved away or left, another one appeared to take his or her place.

Dr. Bussell said one hundred people were sufficient, and that seemed to be the attendance, even though there was never a limit. He wanted to be available to help each individual, personally, through counsel, meditation, healing, or wherever and whatever their need. He stressed personal accountability, responsibility, and not depending on him or any other teacher. From the Essene teachings, I learned that taking responsibility was the first awakening of the soul.

I asked Dr. Bussell about his trip to Mount Carmel, a monastery atop the 1,700-foot-high limestone mountain in Israel where he studied the records of the Essenes. He said, "What makes you think I went *physically?*"

Dr. Bussell explained his ability to enter a state of consciousness where he could read the Akashic Records—a universal filing system of past, present, and future. They are the soul's journey over time. Each soul has its own Akashic Record, and there are collective records of all souls or all journeys. *Aka* is a Tibetan word that means space, storage place, or repository, and *Sa* means sky, hidden, or secret. The Akashic Records have been referred to as the Eternal Book of Life, the Cosmic Mind, the Universal Mind, the Collective Unconscious, or the Collective Subconscious.

Dr. Bussell said, "As the third eye is opened, we can see and read every thought, word, and action that has made an impression on the Akashic Records—the tapestry of life."

Therefore, Dr. Bussell could read documents, such as the history of the Essenes, without needing them, physically, in his presence. "Every being in the universe contributes to and can access the Akashic Records. Because we are all created by and connected to the energy of love, our divine birthright includes having access to the divine wisdom and knowledge contained in the Akashic Records. The flashes of intuition and knowing hunches that we experience every day are glimpses into the divine wisdom contained in the Akashic Records."

I further learned that Dr. Bussell was also able to utilize a technique known as Astral Travel, where he would leave his physical body and travel to another place. To my surprise, I observed this happening on a Sunday lesson when Dr. Bussell suddenly became still, frozen in place. We all wondered what had happened to him and what to do as we turned to each other in wonderment, wanting to offer assistance. In a few minutes, he became animated and remarked, "I went to Lincoln, Nebraska, where I helped the minister make his transition to the other side of life."

The church in Lincoln, Nebraska, was a branch of Chirothesia, and Dr. Bussell chose the minister for this position. At the very moment that Dr. Bussell seemed to freeze in place in church, the minister (in Nebraska) was in the transition process from the physical body into a spiritual expression of life.

Dr. Bussell had the miraculous ability to be wherever you needed him. One night at the restaurant where he worked, Robert had to lock the wine cellar before he could leave. He turned and closed the wrought iron door, and it locked before he realized he had dropped the keys on the floor inside the wine cellar. He had no way of retrieving the keys, and he could not leave the restaurant.

It was two o'clock in the morning, and there were no cell phones in 1963. The day manager would not be there until the next morning. Robert was mildly frantic. What could he do?

Robert remembered what Dr. Bussell had taught us and silently asked for assistance, hoping he could help in this situation. Robert stood for two or three minutes with his eyes closed in total silence. It seemed like an eternity. He thought he heard a click, opened his eyes, put his hand gently on the iron doorknob, and tried to turn it. To his surprise, the knob turned—and the door opened. Later, Dr. Bussell confirmed that he had heard Robert's plea and unlocked the door, without ever physically being there. This kind of miraculous help continued day after day with everyone in the church.

Dr. Bussell was a very generous, giving man, but he was also a very private man. He shared very little of his personal life. However, as our weekly lessons continued, I learned more about him. He was born on November 21, 1882, in Mitchell County, Kansas, and then he moved to Verna, Utah, where he practiced law. In 1919, he moved to Colton, California, and then to Long Beach, where he sold real estate. He was also a corporate constitutional attorney and part of the team of attorneys who established the "In God We Trust" motto on United States currency. He impressed upon us that it was necessary to keep this on our currency to remember to trust God for abundance—and not for the instrument representing wealth and possession. There was no end to my amazement of his enlightened being.

He had many influential friends, one of whom he discussed in a lesson on Sunday, April 5, 1959. He said, "I do not know how many of you knew Theodore Roosevelt. He was a very close friend of mine, a man who was as real as anyone could possibly be, and I was very grateful for his close friendship."

It's been rumored that Theodore Roosevelt's famous quote, "Speak softly and carry a big stick" came from Dr. Bussell. In fact, he demonstrated this part of his personality with one of his neighbors. It seems as though his neighbor, who lived across the street, parked his car halfway over Dr. Bussell's driveway every day, blocking the exit. Each day, Dr. Bussell went across the street to kindly ask the man if he would move his car so he could back out. The man would always comply, but he continued parking halfway in his driveway each day. One morning, Dr. Bussell came out, and with no emotion, got into his car, put it in reverse, and went sailing down the driveway into the parked car. The man never parked there again!

While practicing law in 1917, Dr. Bussell met Dr. W. Grant Hess, an osteopathic doctor who hired him to write the incorporation papers for the Chirothesian Church in Los Angeles. Dr. Hess recognized Dr. Bussell's potential, and from their association, Dr. Bussell joined with Dr. Hess in the teaching of Chirothesia. *Chiro* means hand; *Theos* means God. *Chirothesia* is a Greek word that means "healing by God's hand."

Dr. Hess and Dr. Bussell incorporated the Chirothesian Church of Faith, Inc., in California, on August 2, 1917. Dr. Bussell explained that Chirothesia is based on the four gospels of Matthew, Mark, Luke, and John. In this sense, Chirothesia is entirely Christian in its teaching, tenets, and beliefs. A Chirothesian is one who daily practices the Universal Laws of God and parallels the Essene teachings.

The Chirothesian Church was established legally in order to also serve as protection for healers. It was also the Chirothesian Institute for Chiropractors and later became the National Academy of Metaphysics, an eight-course study written by Dr. Bussell.

By 1952, when I was attending the Chirothesian Church regularly, I was surprised to learn that Dr. Bussell did not advertise, commercialize, or proselytize, yet so many people, including famous people, attended. Chirothesia was a teaching ahead of its time, which did not make it popular or even welcomed in various circles. Spiritual healings were not generally accepted, so everyone was careful not to broadcast that healings were taking place in the Chirothesian Church; however, many medical doctors cooperated with Dr. Bussell.

You often hear stories about people and miraculous events, but you may have doubts about what you hear. I was no different. I wanted proof. Well, after eight years, I got it! I couldn't deny the results I saw. I am so blessed to have been in Dr. Bussell's presence and to have witnessed the amazing transformations in people's lives that took place every day.

Dr. Bussell was so connected to the Infinite that when he visualized a perfect body or incident, it manifested. When he visualized himself in a different location, he was there. It was obvious that he came to show us how to think and live the Universal Laws. He was my perfect role model: a quiet, gentle, humble, loving man who did not want recognition. I tried to thank him many times for a healing or help I received, but he simply replied, "Oh, please don't thank me. I didn't do anything. Thank God."

And I did. Dr. Bussell exemplified the truth and lived the Essene motto: *By your fruits, ye shall know them.*

CHAPTER 3

Surgery or Healing

At times in our lives, we may be confronted with the question: *Shall I have a traditional operation or try the more alternative, natural way of healing?*

Approximately a year before we met Dr. Bussell, my husband was scheduled for surgery at the veteran's hospital in the San Fernando Valley for removal of a rectal tumor. Several people familiar with spiritual healing, including our friend Carroll Righter, tried to convince me that Robert should receive a few healing treatments from Dr. Bussell to determine whether surgery was necessary. At the time, I didn't welcome the suggestion. I was afraid to try alternative methods, even though it seemed to work for many others. I hadn't reached that place in consciousness where I believed it would work, and neither had Robert. We weren't open to accepting this kind of experience. Our friends insisted that we would never know for ourselves if we didn't try, claiming that's how they had found out about Dr. Bussell's miraculous healing ability.

Our friends said, "The best way to know what you know is to experience it yourself."

They also said, "Seeing is believing."

We decided to learn all we could about these healing treatments. First, we looked through lessons from Dr. Bussell's course on spiritual healing and found:

> Healing is not a special gift for special people. It's open and available to all of us. It is an infinite gift of the Life Force. The world of electricity will not light a house unless the house itself is prepared to receive that electricity, so the infinite and eternal power that we call God cannot help us unless we are prepared to receive that within ourselves. How much of this Life Force can we accept? An instant healing is possible when you are totally receptive and believe. If not, it may take a little longer. The Master Jesus could heal instantly, because people totally accepted and believed. However, Jesus couldn't heal those who weren't ready for this miraculous action. If I handed you a check for a million dollars, it wouldn't be yours until you actually accepted it. So, what is a miracle? Miracles are nothing more or less than the enfoldment of the Natural Law. "What you believe, you can conceive." Healing can be instantaneous. "We can heal as quickly as we can accept the healing. The actual time it takes to believe and accept is the enfoldment of this wonderful Universal Law in action. There is no time in Mind."

In addition, Dr. Bussell taught that:

> The cells of our body do not transmit; they only receive. If you keep saying you have a headache, the body will respond to your thought and you will be rewarded with a headache.

I tested this Natural Universal Law once when I concentrated my thoughts on having a sore throat. Two days later, I experienced a sore throat. I used the same law of thought to eliminate it, but it took a little longer than it did to materialize. It's easier to think negatively because we are used to it, but it takes more energy to think positively. I enjoyed the process of experimenting and proving this to myself. This made me wonder if our fleeting, frightening, random thoughts created everything we think about. Dr. Bussell had a perfect explanation for this. He said, "We were saved because we didn't think any thought long enough."

Just imagine what would happen if everything we thought about materialized all at once! Thank God that it doesn't.

The more I learned from Dr. Bussell, the more I realized that if life is a school, I had just begun to learn how to think. According to Dr. Bussell, one of humanity's largest lessons is to learn how to discern right from wrong, or creative from destructive action.

Before Robert made the final decision about the healing, we discussed and questioned the healing treatments with our friends and family. Dr. Bussell's secretary sympathized with our dilemma and offered her help by inviting us to come into the main sanctuary to watch a private healing take place.

A young man had a collapsed lung due to a cleat spike and puncture that occurred when he played football. His chest had been caved in for several years, and it was difficult for him to breathe. Anyone observing him could easily detect he had a problem breathing. He experienced several healing treatments from Dr. Bussell before he would accept the healing, and this day was the culmination of those treatments.

Robert and I were instructed to stand quietly in back of the sanctuary to watch the healing process. The man was in front of the room when Dr. Bussell entered. He stood behind the man, leaned forward, and whispered in his ear. Dr. Bussell closed his eyes and uttered a prayer.

It was a very tense moment for Robert and me. I was afraid to breathe, fearing I would disturb the atmosphere. Neither of us moved a muscle. I could see the man was apprehensive, but he was clearly demonstrating acceptance and belief.

Dr. Bussell then performed a "laying on of hands," which is a means of receiving the Holy Spirit that has healing properties. Dr. Bussell placed his hands under the front of the young man's ribcage and asked him to take a slow, deep breath. More chills ran through my body as I watched the man inhale—his chest expanded fully— as he appeared to breathe normally for the first time in years. We were relieved! The man was overjoyed and had tears in his eyes.

I was still breathless from suspense and anticipation, but I was so grateful for the opportunity to witness this miraculous action. This amazing healing made a strong impression upon me. I was certain Dr. Bussell was a remarkable and gifted healer, and Robert agreed. As a consequence of this demonstration of healing, Robert consented to have several healing treatments. We wondered how many he would need, and why one person needed five treatments, while others needed only three. How is the number determined? Dr. Bussell explained that he would observe the thoughts of the person who needed the healing. If the person thought and believed he needed four treatments to be healed, Dr. Bussell would give him or her four treatments. Due to the person's belief, after the fourth treatment, the healing took place.

I asked, "What makes the healings possible?"

Dr. Bussell answered, in a warm loving tone, "The law of health is perfect, radiant, and dynamic. I don't see or know anything else. Whatever interferes with the natural flow of energy, I see as removed. It just doesn't exist because we are created in the image and likeness of our creator. The things that are not harmonious with the body and not perfect don't belong there."

I asked how long it would take to let go of negative thoughts or reach that place in consciousness where we know only perfection since not everyone is the same.

Dr. Bussell replied, "All the flowers in the garden don't bloom at the same time. The time is different for each person. No two things in the universe are identical."

Upon completion of his healing treatments, Robert asked Dr. Bussell if he should keep his scheduled surgery appointment at the hospital.

Dr. Bussell said, "Oh, yes, Mr. Gaard. I would if I were you."

Robert packed his bag for the trip to the hospital and said it wasn't necessary for me to be there until he completed the routine examination required prior to the operation. He said he would call me as soon as he confirmed the time of the surgery.

I anxiously awaited his call and was ready to leave at a moment's notice. I was amazed when two hours later, Robert drove up the driveway to our home. I met him at the door, with surprise. "What are you doing here?" I exclaimed.

He was full of mixed feelings and looked confused and relieved. "As I finished the paperwork, they called me into the exam room, and I was placed on the table. The doctor examined me, and with a puzzled look, said the same thing to me as you just did: *What are you doing here?* I told him I was there for the removal of a tumor. I felt exasperated and asked, "Wasn't it on the chart?" However, regardless of what my record stated, the doctor shrugged and said, 'Sorry, we can't find anything here. You might as well go home.'"

Facing each other, and still standing in the doorway, I took a deep breath, smiled, gasped, and tightly hugged Robert with gratitude. "Wasn't that fantastic news?" I exclaimed.

We now had the faith we needed that we could contact our loving Dr. Bussell by telephone and explain our illness or discomfort, and within minutes, the condition disappeared. If we saw him in person, he gave us his laying on of hands treatment. He said, "The laying on of hands isn't necessary, but some people want the personal contact."

As time passed, I witnessed tumors, birthmarks, epilepsy, and fevers disappear almost instantly. Other forms of illness or disease were also cured; however, you seldom believe anything until you have had the experience yourself. I was blessed with the opportunity to appreciate both seeing and experiencing it. If anyone made a request for a healing, it was accomplished, either personally or in absentia. Dr. Bussell's mind was so linked to the Infinite Source that when he visualized a perfect body or outcome, it manifested.

Upon returning to Dr. Bussell's classes, I was curious about one thing. "Dr. Bussell," I asked, "I don't understand. Why did you tell Robert to go ahead with the surgery appointment when you knew he was cured?"

With an amused smile, he replied, "Robert needed to see the proof."

He was right. And I guess I needed it too.

CHAPTER 4

Healing with Light

What does "healing is not possible beyond the point of no return" mean? It means that the disease would destroy too much of the body to be healed if not acted upon in the beginning stages. Dr. Bussell had stressed healing is possible, providing it is done before the "point of no return."

Why do we continue not to face the issue? Procrastination seems to be a widespread universal problem. Since we don't want to know or hear any bad news, we just pretend it doesn't exist. We would rather ignore it and hope it will go away. I know because I did just that and paid the price of having to undergo an operation I didn't want.

If we don't want a healing, all we have to do is deny it. If we deny a condition, we have to accept that a condition exists in order to deny it. But, in the Universal Law of Health, there is only one degree of health, and that is perfect health. In the Universal Law of Health, there is no denial. There is no room in God's law for denial. There is only the recognition of the Truth. The truth in health is that we are created to be and have a birthright of radiant, vital, and dynamic health.

Approximately thirty-four years after Dr. Bussell made his transition, I felt a pain in my right breast. Even though I intuitively knew better, I refused to recognize the condition. I waited a year before I did anything about it. I was too busy, and I kept saying it didn't exist. I did the one thing I was told not to do: I denied it. *It will go away. It can't be anything serious.*

Almost a year passed from the onset of the initial symptom before I was awakened in the night by a distinctly, crystal-clear voice inside of my head. "You haven't much more time." I was shocked! Needless to say, I didn't sleep the rest of the night. *What do I do now? Have I waited too long?*

I went through the procedure, the X-ray, biopsy, etc. The results revealed there was a cancerous tumor in my right breast, known as ductal carcinoma in situ or DCIS. After much counseling, an operation was scheduled at UCLA. The surgery went smoothly and quickly. I had a wonderful Vietnamese doctor, and she said I could go home immediately following the operation. I was so relieved, grateful, and happy to hear the outcome was successful and no remaining disease tissue was present. Even though the doctor informed me that all disease had been removed, I was bombarded with professional advice about having radiation and chemotherapy in order to ward off the return of the disease.

Naturally, I refused. Because of my teaching, I believed I could be healed without further medical intervention. Now, I reasoned, I must practice what I learned about healing, and be the example to prove it is true. Therefore, I continued in daily meditations, thanking God for my perfect healing. Everything went well. Annual mammograms were clear, and my health proved to be excellent. A few years later, the seed of fear and doubt that had been planted by many people, who were continuously saying, "It will return," manifested. The cancer returned. I was disappointed in myself for carrying the thought and believing the prediction.

The year was 1996 and still, the healing practice of laying on of hands was not widely recognized or utilized. I decided I could overcome the cancer if only I had help. Since Dr. Bussell had made the transition, I called my assistant, who was a skilled meditator, trained and experienced in the healing technique of Chirothesia. We began twice-a-week treatments of Laying on of Hands and daily meditation using the application of light to facilitate a perfect healing.

Light plays a very important part in healing and has been utilized in many instances. The Bible tells us that God said, "Let there be light." Light is still here since the beginning of time. In fact, laser light instruments are used in healing wounds, treating pain, skin abrasions, corrective eye surgery, and many other types of surgery. What technology can attain today through laser light, we can also accomplish with our thoughts by simply surrounding an area that needs healing with a field of light.

I increased my treatments to three times a week and continued until I thought I had been healed. The time came, and my assistant accompanied me to the doctor's office. We waited patiently for the verdict. I closed my eyes and prayed that the physician would find nothing and I was completely healed.

After the extensive examination, the doctor smiled and said, "You're clear. You can go now. I detect no sign of the cancer."

We knew this would be the verdict, but it was such a relief to hear it confirmed.

It appears that after we learn a truth, the Universal Law gives us an opportunity to prove it. It seems I passed another test to see how much faith I was capable of demonstrating. At that point, I made up my mind to never allow fear or doubt to get in the way of what I know to be true.

We can do things to deface the body, but in order to restore it to health we have to recognize and correct our mistakes in wrong thoughts and actions. We need to acknowledge the magnificent power that created everything perfect. When we think and know only perfection, without a shadow of a doubt, the cells of the body will react according to our thoughts and return to their original states.

The Presence, God, Force, or Infinite, doesn't know illness. This Presence only knows perfection because everything was created perfect. There is no room for recognition of pain or suffering, so the Presence doesn't know you have a pain in your head, back, foot, or any other part of the body. It would be ridiculous to pray to remove one of those conditions because the Presence doesn't know anything about it. How can that Presence do something of which it knows nothing? So, what do we do when we need healing? We simply recognize the Divine Presence and Power of Universal Law, which is perfection. We must express heartfelt gratitude for perfect healing taking place now, and we must let go.

I was fortunate to also witness the power of healing light on Carroll Righter. It was exciting to actually witness what light could do with someone you know and see almost every day.

One morning, Robert and I were having breakfast with Carroll in his sunroom, when, out of the blue, Carroll began complaining about the large round brown mole on the end of his nose. Carroll's career was on the brink of skyrocketing and he was about to have his first television appearance. He was famous, but some people had never seen his face before. He said he needed to look his best, and the brown mole was just too prominent. He had used makeup and bleaching cream, but nothing seemed to eliminate the dark brown spot that he had acquired from too much sunbathing.

Carroll decided he'd better get in touch with Dr. Bussell and see what he should do about it. I know he contacted Dr. Bussell because two days later, Carroll called me on the phone in peals of laughter. He said he went into the bathroom, looked twice in the mirror, and after a double take, he discovered a very shiny white nose. He said, "You must come over and see for yourself." I couldn't wait to run over to make sure he wasn't kidding. We had a good laugh, examining his white, shiny nose. The mole was completely gone!

How did Dr. Bussell do this? It's actually quite simple. He used the same Universal Principle. We live in a world of opposites. If you have a glass of dirty water and pour bleach in it, the water becomes clear. If you want something dark to change to light, you must see in your mind's eye, only white. The atoms will change according to your power of concentrated thought. Of course, being a little more evolved might help, such as knowing how to master your thoughts.

Naturally, Carroll called Dr. Bussell to thank him and tell him that not only had the brown mole disappeared, but also his nose was the whitest and shiniest it had ever been.

Dr. Bussell said, "Oh dear, I must have used too much light!"

CHAPTER 5

From Blindness to Sight

By then, I was not surprised by anything that took place with regard to miraculous events in the lives of people who were surrounding Dr. Bussell.

When we first met, he said, "If you want action, you'll find it here."

I found out life certainly wasn't dull in Chirothesia. Every day with each experience, either personally witnessed or overheard, was a new and exciting awakening.

At a Sunday service on April 2, 1956, I discovered something fascinating about Dr. Bussell. He had been blind for four years! In the midst of the service, he explained the cause of his blindness. He said, "I had done some work I should not have done, for I could not delegate it to someone else; therefore, I simply lost the power of sight."

During his blindness, a young woman was taking care of him in a facility. He did not name the location of the facility, but he did mention that there was a budding rosebush outside his window. He said he had all the faith that he would see again. He looked forward to his daily encounter with the young caretaker who faithfully followed his request, reporting to him the progress of the unfolding rose, each and every day. He had secretly made up his mind that by the time the rose opened to its fullest beauty, he would regain his sight.

On Easter morning, March 27, 1921, the rose burst into full bloom. When he was told the rose had bloomed, he asked to be taken to the window. Upon opening his eyes, he realized his prayers had been answered. He had never seen such a beautiful rose. He said, "When we pass through darkness, we appreciate the light that much more."

Everyone listened intently as he related the remainder of the story in full detail.

> Being deprived of the beauty of the world is not a blessed experience; when blindness did come, I was not happier with it than you or anyone else might be, left in utter darkness. That, however, is all past now, and that experience has probably been my greatest blessing in all my life—not the fact that I was deprived of the beauty of sight, but that I learned something to do to reestablish my sight. That was a tremendous blessing, and I am very grateful for it. But the greatest blessing is the fact that I realized within myself that the unity with God was never broken, was always there, and I realized that I could have my sight again. I did receive my sight, and it is a tremendous blessing. I think I see as well as the average person, possibly better than many. But that in itself is not really important. The important thing is the lesson I learned from having the recovery of sight. Sight was natural, and as soon as I got myself back into perfect harmony, my sight was reestablished. People who knew me while I was blind, and know me

now, realize that something very much worthwhile took place. It has been somewhat of an inspiration to them, for they saw what to them was Truth in action.

People who knew Dr. Bussell, and had attended his services longer than Robert and I, knew of his healings and believed he was demonstrating the truth that with God, all things are possible. Robert and I, however, were inquisitive. Perhaps we needed further proof of Dr. Bussell's miraculous recovery from blindness. When we noticed that Dr. Bussell wore reading glasses, we quickly located his optometrist and scheduled an eye examination for Robert.

During the examination, Robert casually asked the optometrist if he knew Dr. Bussell. Of course, it was confirmed. The optometrist had examined Dr. Bussell's eyes after he had regained his sight. As far as the optometrist could see, the retinas were detached in both eyes. He couldn't figure out how Dr. Bussell could possibly see anything out of his eyes. Furthermore, at that time, there was no operation for connecting a detached retina. Regardless of his findings, the optometrist fitted Dr. Bussell for reading glasses, but he was completely puzzled about anyone's ability to see in spite of the medical facts presented.

The encounter with the optometrist gave me some answers, but it also created more questions. I had to find out how Dr. Bussell could see. On the following Sunday morning, I approached him after the service and asked him to explain how he could see with a detached retina.

He said, "Well, the Law of Aerodynamics says that the bumblebee cannot fly because his little body is too heavy for its tiny wings, but the bumblebee doesn't know about the Law of Aerodynamics. He only knows about God's law, and he goes ahead and flies anyway."

Well, of course, it was clear to me that Dr. Bussell was living God's Law, which restored his sight. Nothing was unusual where miracles were concerned. It was a joy for me to know and see the Truth in action. This eliminates all fear. "Perfect love casteth out all fear." I John 4:18

Dr. Bussell wanted to be available to all of us within the congregation in case we ever needed help. In other words, when in need, we could call him mentally for help, and there would be an almost immediate response and change in a situation. Many times, help would come without the thought. He was so in tune with everyone that he knew when something wasn't right, and he would immediately visualize the appropriate action to remedy the situation.

In 1954, I met Mrs. Bailey, a very sweet elderly lady, who, despite her blindness, was a talented pianist. She came to Dr. Bussell for healing treatments, and he placed his hand over her eyes for a period of a few months. One day, Mrs. Bailey opened her eyes and was able to see. Although she would have to wear glasses to enhance her vision, Mrs. Bailey's blindness was cured. Mrs. Bailey was overjoyed and wanted to contribute to the church. Since she had very little income, her gift of gratitude was to play the piano in church every Sunday, or whenever Dr. Bussell required her services. With her new gift of vision, she also transcribed his lessons and helped in the office.

One afternoon when Mrs. Bailey left the church, she began crossing the street at Normandie and Hollywood Boulevard, and the driver of an approaching car ran the red light. The car struck Mrs. Bailey and knocked her across the intersection to the opposite side of the street. Normally, she would have been killed, but Dr. Bussell, with his clairvoyant sight, saw what was happening. Being in tune with Mrs. Bailey's vibration, yet still physically at church, Dr. Bussell extended a mental projection of himself between Mrs. Bailey and the car. Mrs. Bailey was hospitalized for a couple of days, but she soon returned to playing the piano and helping in the office.

Meanwhile, since Dr. Bussell had "placed" himself in front of the approaching car, his physical body suffered pain from the impact. This was a lesson in self-projection. The consequences of Dr. Bussell's healings, however, never stopped him from healing those who needed him.

As powerful as my Master teacher Dr. Bussell was, he also had initiations to go through before he became the true Master. We all go through initiations every day, whether we are aware of it or not: making the right decisions in a crisis, choosing the right workplace, rising above an argument, or changing an opinion we've had for years that simply wasn't right for us. All of these situations remove a layer of confusion or darkness from our minds to let the light of truth shine through. This initiates us into a higher level of understanding, knowledge, and experience.

Dr. Bussell wanted to know if he had passed the initiations in this life to warrant his Mastership. He projected that thought into the Presence and later—as he explained it—he walked into his room and a scarab stone was suspended in midair, the symbol of Eternal Life and representing Mastership. He was overcome with joy and his heart was filled with gratitude. The stone was set in a ring for his little finger. The ring was very special, and he never failed to wear it. When I shook his hand, I could feel the power emanating from this ring, even before I knew what it meant to him.

Years later, when Dr. Bussell made the transition, the ring was on his finger, as it had always been, but the stone was gone. It simply dematerialized back into the ethers from whence it came.

There is a key to the miraculous manifestations that take place in life. It is having faith and gratitude, but most of all, love.

CHAPTER 6

The Invisible Presence

How many times have you been aware of an Invisible Presence that saved you from an accident, held you back from falling, or stopped other impending dangers?

Have you noticed there is an Invisible Presence guiding and protecting you, whether you know it or not? You may not see it, but many times you are aware of it.

Recently, I read a story in the newspaper about a six-year-old girl who was standing on the back fender of the family's SUV when her mother and father drove away without realizing she was there. People in passing vehicles were frantically shouting and trying to signal the father, that the little girl was on the back, holding on for her life. Several blocks later, the father finally realized what was happening, and he gradually and carefully pulled the SUV over and stopped. The little girl's mother jumped out—her heart beating furiously—as she grabbed her daughter and held her in her arms.

The little girl turned calmly to her mother and said, "Oh, it's all right, Mommy. I was safe. There was an angel beside me, telling me she would help me hold tight so I would be safe."

Children, because they are true believers are able to connect easily with the Invisible Presence. We, as adults, are often too busy in the material world to connect or even recognize that the Presence is all around us. The Invisible Presence takes different forms. In the aforementioned case, the little girl saw an angel, which was visible only to her. In my experience, the Invisible Presence has appeared many times in various forms.

Once it appeared in the form of a homeless man who rang my doorbell and wanted nothing but to alert me that I had left my keys in the door. For me, this was a lesson never to be disregarded. We are not all what we appear to be. The Presence has even appeared to me in the form of a scent. When I find myself overwhelmed with life's problems, I am suddenly engulfed by a wonderful fragrance that follows me wherever I go—even in my sleep. After a few days, the scent disappears, leaving me with the assurance that I am loved. Help and support is all around me—all I have to do is accept it.

But the most dramatic of all my experiences was when the Invisible Presence appeared to me in the form of a sound. In 1976, my husband Robert had just passed away, leaving me alone with our sixteen-year-old daughter and what felt like a huge, empty house, complete with huge bills. One night, as I was tossing and turning in bed, fighting with myself to get some rest, I heard several voices in the other room. I was terrified at first, but as I listened carefully, it seemed there was a meeting taking place. Even though I couldn't make out what I was hearing, a feeling of comfort and peace came over me. It was as if angels were there to watch over me. I slept like a baby that night. From then on, I knew that everything would be all right when night came and I heard the voices.

Dr. Bussell was able to connect with the Invisible Presence, and he was able to use the Presence and transfer the energy to other places and people so that they could experience the Invisible Presence too. This was felt many times by many people.

I remember one day when Tila, Marguerite, and Betty, three women in their fifties, were bursting with excitement as they told me of their plans to take a summer vacation and drive back to the Midwest to see relatives. They were confident about making the trip, but they felt apprehensive about their old automobile that wasn't in very good condition.

After much discussion, they decided to ask Dr. Bussell if he would please assist and pray that they would reach their destination without problems. They knew if he was praying, they would be safe. Even though he was very busy giving healings from six in the morning until ten at night, he agreed to help. So, with his blessing, they started on their journey across the California desert from Los Angeles to Blythe. It was a hot day in August, and in the 1950s, air conditioning was non-existent in cars. So you can imagine how uncomfortably hot it was to drive across the desert.

They planned to leave early in the morning when it was cooler and stop when they reached the nearest town—around noon. The first day was uneventful, but on the second day of driving through the vast, dry desert, they developed a problem. The horn began honking uncontrollably, and there was nothing they could do to make it stop. They were afraid to stop the car for fear that it wouldn't start up again. What would they do? Imagine three mature women alone in the desert in the 1950s with zero knowledge of how a car even functions. They could stop and raise the hood to attract travelers, but there were very few cars making a trip across the desert in the blistering heat. The only reasonable solution was to drive to the nearest town as quickly as possible to find a service station. Not knowing the cause of the problem and being limited financially, they were in turmoil. Eventually, they made it to a service station in Blythe. They were anxious to hear the diagnosis, but the mechanic asked, "Ladies, how long have you been driving this car?"

"Since we left Los Angeles a couple of days ago. Why do you ask?" Tila replied.

"Well, you've got a loose wire that would have set your car on fire if it had touched anything," he answered.

Needless to say, all three women were shocked to hear this. All they could think of was the car bursting into flames! What a close call! They were relieved to be safe and sound. The mechanic was baffled and couldn't explain why the horn had been stuck, honking away. The loose wire had nothing to do with the horn.

As soon as they regained their composure, the women knew exactly whom to thank for the Invisible Presence … Dr. Bussell. When they asked him why the horn had honked, Dr. Bussell said with a smile, "Well, *we* had to do something to get your attention."

There are so many stories that I couldn't possibly relate all of them, but one about a missing diamond made quite a lasting impression. One afternoon, Dr. Bussell received a phone call from Vera Teasdale, wife of the movie actor Adolf Menjou. Vera was frantic as she explained that the diamond was missing from the setting in her engagement ring. She knew it was somewhere in the house, and she had to find it before Adolf came home from the studio. If she didn't find it, he would be livid. It was a very large and expensive diamond, and she couldn't fathom it being lost.

Dr. Bussell responded to her call by advising her to remain calm and alert, and he assured her that she would find it. She went about the house, remaining alert, and continued to scan each room. She looked all day, but when the day was nearly over, she became discouraged and gave up looking. Full of worry, she wondered how she would tell Adolf that the precious diamond was missing?

She reluctantly entered the master bedroom to change for dinner when her eye caught something black in the corner of the thick white carpet. Cautiously, she approached and gazed at the floor where she discovered something that looked like black material placed on the carpet. When she came closer, the shining diamond was in the center of the black material.

"Oh my word!" she exclaimed in joyful surprise. She immediately called to thank Dr. Bussell, but she wondered how the diamond had gotten there. When she asked why it was on a piece of black material in the corner of the bedroom, Dr. Bussell said said, "Since you have a white carpet, Mrs. Menjou, I thought it would be easier for you to locate."

The manifestation of the diamond on the black material was beyond my comprehension, and I had to ask Dr. Bussell how he did it. He answered, "The first thing I did was to see the diamond in all of its size and brilliance. Once I had that clearly in mind, I mentally created a piece of black material and placed the diamond in a spot where I knew she would find it—in the corner of the master bedroom."

Was it really that easy? Yes and no. It's not easy to focus and concentrate all of our energy on a particular subject, but when we do, we can create as easily as Dr. Bussell did. We are all in the process of monitoring our thoughts. The secret is to know that you can do it without a shadow of a doubt.

When those nagging doubts come crawling back, how do you get rid of them? We can do this by practicing patience and a daily devotion to the faith in knowing the Truth and how it works. There is an immutable law, and once you know it, you can do anything, within reason. It must be for the good of all, or it won't work. The law says, "What you send forth comes back tenfold." If you give love, love returns to you. If you give kindness, kindness returns to you. If you give charity, charity returns to you. This is the way to complete success.

As I mentioned before, all of the little miracles were a daily occurrence during my time with Dr. Bussell, and it was no surprise when another one took place.

For several years, Carroll Righter had been renting a lovely old furnished home in Hollywood on Franklin Avenue while the owners traveled in Europe. Carroll conducted all of his business appointments and social parties at this house, and everything he ever needed was there. It was conveniently located and easy to find for everyone who wished to see him. We were there so much it felt like our home as well. Since this home is where Carroll had his monthly astrological parties, honoring the movie stars on their birthday, it also became a famous place. You can imagine what a shock it was when the owners of the house returned from Europe and notified Carroll that they were planning to sell the house.

Losing the house would be a great loss to Carroll since all of his clients, both in the United States and abroad, were familiar with this home, which he affectionately called Harmony House. Carroll had heard through the grapevine that there were already two offers on the house for more than he could afford, and he called Dr. Bussell and told him about his dilemma.

Dr. Bussell simply said, "Present your offer, and allow God to do the rest."

The owners contacted Carroll, revealing the details of other, higher offers and explained why they wanted to accept them. It was a tremendously tense situation for Carroll, and it was a very difficult decision for the owners, especially since Carroll had been such a good tenant for many years.

After pondering all the offers for several days, the owners made their decision. Despite the higher offers, they chose to accept Carroll Righter's ridiculously low offer. They didn't even know why they chose Carroll's offer! It certainly was much easier and less complicated since Carroll loved the house, complete with all the furnishings, and the owners did not want the hassle of a big move.

It is amazing what prayer can do! Dr. Bussell said he merely saw Carroll with the deed in his hand, living happily in the home.

In Dr. Bussell's meditation, he knew the outcome, without a shadow of a doubt, and his expectation was "large." According to him, in placing any situation in "Right Action," you must remember to see the outcome in a positive light. It must be for the highest good of all. Otherwise, you are not in harmony with the Universal Law, and there may be an uncomfortable lesson to learn.

The power of positive thought can manifest the outcome you desire, providing it passes the following three steps:

1. Is it good for me?
2. Is it good for the other person (or persons)?
3. Does it hurt anyone?

If the desired outcome answers the first and second questions with a yes and the third with a no, you are in harmony with the Universal Law. In meditating on the right and perfect outcome, you release it to the Power and Presence for Right Action, setting God's love in motion, and it is done.

CHAPTER 7

Proving Your Love

What is this thing called love? Everybody is looking for love in any person, place, or thing and wants to know what love is or what it isn't. The best way to learn about love is by example, and our teacher was the best example. Every time you read a book, hear a lecture, or go to a class on love, you are told that learning how to love is the reason why we are here in this lifetime. They all say that love is the answer to how you change your life, your health, and your relationships.

A surprise experience demonstrated the real power of love on a Friday afternoon when we were sitting in church. Around 3:30 in the midst of a lesson, we heard the door in back of the church open quietly. Surprised, I looked over my shoulder to see who entered because no one ever came late to a class. When I glanced in back, I saw a tall young man, who was not well dressed, standing at the side of the door. His behavior didn't give any indication that he intended to come in to sit down. I felt a little uneasy and wondered what Dr. Bussell was going to do.

Dr. Bussell continued quietly for a few minutes and suddenly stopped talking, and closed his eyes momentarily as if in meditation. We knew something wasn't right, but we just waited. In a few seconds, we heard the door open quietly and close again. I turned to look and noticed the man had left as quietly as he had come. A few moments into the lesson, Dr. Bussell explained to us that the young man who entered the church had just robbed the bank on the corner and simply came in to hide from the police. Dr. Bussell said he gave him instructions by implanting the thought in his mind to give himself up because it would be easier for him if he did. The man complied with this inner direction and turned himself in to the police because Dr. Bussell showered him with so much love that he had the courage to carry out the right action.

An intense thought of love from your heart can be as powerful as any action. I'm sure you have felt surrounded with love at some time in your life, and it felt very real. When we are lonely or overwhelmed, we can recall the moments when we received intense love and felt fulfilled. No matter what we are doing, love will fill the need. I often look back on a day when I unexpectedly received intense love.

It was 1964; Robert had taken our four-year-old daughter for a walk. I was so busy and preoccupied with counseling people out of our home. It was a relief to have time to work by myself. I was relaxed and started getting some work done, but I heard the door unlock after only a half hour. It couldn't possibly be Robert returning. I had specifically asked him to keep Greta busy for at least a few hours so that I could finish something without interruption, which was never easy with a four-year-old running around.

I was disappointed when I heard their voices and realized my "alone time" was over. As I walked to meet them, with an unpleasant attitude and perhaps a snide remark, Greta came running toward me. She had the brightest smile and held up her little hand filled with flowers. "I picked these for you, Mommy!" she said with joy.

For a moment, I thought my heart had stopped, and maybe it did. Maybe the whole world stopped so that I could remember that moment of pure love. Not only had I just received such intense love from Greta, but there was a sudden outburst of love that poured from me as well. Robert apologized for not giving me enough time alone, but he explained that Greta just couldn't wait to bring the pretty flowers home to Mommy.

I smiled and thanked Robert for bringing Greta home at that moment. The experience far surpassed any desire to complete a task. This memory is as fresh in my mind as the day it happened, and I am thankful for it.

To me, the most beautiful act of proving love came from the real events in the life of Dr. and Mrs. Bussell. Dr. Bussell loved his wife dearly, like no other, and the following is an example of how he proved his love for her. I'm wondering how many of us could do the same.

From the moment he saw her, Dr. Bussell knew he had been with Josephine during many lifetimes, and it wasn't long before he asked her to marry him. He knew and remembered the different "parts" they had played together in other lives: an aunt and uncle, a father and daughter, a brother and sister, and more. From their association and love for each other, this lifetime could culminate in a marriage. This would be their last incarnation together.

Mrs. Bussell had lost her first husband to a terminal illness, and loving her children unconditionally, she knew the financial burden had fallen upon her shoulders. Being a responsible mother, she became a seamstress and did everything she could to fulfill her children's needs and take care of her family. When she met Dr. Bussell, she felt in her heart that he should not be financially responsible for the care of her children. Though she truly loved him, she refused marriage until her children were grown and able to support and care for themselves. This didn't seem to put a strain on their relationship, even though Dr. Bussell had to patiently wait fifteen years before he could marry the love of his life.

After years of marriage, their love grew deeper, but Mrs. Bussell became weary of waiting for Dr. Bussell to return home from his tireless work. Because of his love and devotion to his work, many times he would be giving healing treatments far into the late evening and sometimes not return home until after ten—even though he started his day at sunrise.

Mrs. Bussell was a little woman with a cherub's face, white curly hair, and a very sweet smile. Because of her loving presence, everyone called her, the "Little Queen." One day with her sweet, firm voice, she said, "You are gone so much. You are hardly ever here. I want to know if you really love me."

"Of course," he said with a smile. "More than anything in this world." Like a love story from many lifetimes past, he was putty in her hands.

"Would you prove your love?" she asked sweetly.

"Anything," he said.

"Would you wash the windows?"

"But sweetheart, it's raining."

"But if you love me, you will wash the windows."

Even though he was in his eighties, he was up the ladder within seconds. The raindrops poured down upon his smiling face. You might ask how I know this really happened. I was at the church when he returned, smiling, but rather wet from the rain.

The highest form of love is sacrifice. Sacrifice is when you can give up something you want or treasure to fulfill another's need.

I learned the lesson of sacrifice in 1975 when Robert was diagnosed with pancreatic cancer. He went through an operation, but the disease had metastasized, and there was no hope for recovery. He quickly became very weak, but we had not lost hope. We heard of an alternative treatment for cancer that was only available in Mexico. Every week, I drove Robert from Los Angeles to Mexico for his treatment. I also gave him massages every day, puréed his food, and constantly researched new ways in which to help him through this.

It left little time for myself. In order to meet the demands of my designated schedule, I resorted to eating fast food, living a stressful, harried pace, and not getting enough sleep. My body suffered for it later. I could have resented this intrusion into my life, and asked, "Why me?" Instead, I kept expressing gratitude for the twenty-four years we had together and for the opportunity to show my love and appreciation to Robert, who had supported and supplied my needs on every level of my life.

One year after his diagnosis, Robert passed away. I was so grateful for the truth I had learned to express gratitude for a love instead of sadness or sorrow.

Dr. Bussell gave us an example of this kind of love. He said, "No greater love hath any man than this, that he lay down his life for his friend. Not give it up, but live in such a manner that true unconditional love is expressed in whatever action takes place."

On our journey to enlightenment, there are qualities we must incorporate into our energy field that bring light into our soul: kindness, humility, generosity, sacrifice, selflessness, truth, and love. Love is the basis for every quality, experience, and idea. Love solves our problems in every instance. Without love, there is no Universal Law. The law is love.

At Carroll Righter's traditional Zodiac Party. He would bring live animals each month representing a symbol of the Zodiac. Robert Gaard and Ray.

Carroll and myself in the breakfast room just before he called Dr. Bussell to tell him of the despicable brown mole.

Carroll Righter and the brown mole.

Carroll and me in 1970. We called him "Pappy."

Modeling in the French Room at the Beverly Wilshire Hotel.

On stage in "Kitchen Privileges." The early
part of my career in Los Angeles.

Camp Carson Colorado, singing for the soldiers.

On the stage at camp Carson Colorado,
where I met Robert during the war.

Wedding picture Robert and me, September
17, 1952. Colorado Springs, Colorado.

CHAPTER 8

The Cosmic Law of Abundance

Who doesn't need money? It isn't the money we need; it's the things that money will buy. To many people, peace of mind depends on being financially secure. There never was a need that an abundance didn't exist to fill. Abundance of all things existed before we came to the planet, or we couldn't think of it.

Our money problems are here to help us learn the lesson of faith and trust in the Power greater than ourselves that provides everything. Learning to be in the attitude of abundance is a lesson for all humanity: *how* to receive, *how* to use, and *how* to give.

Our greatest problem is balance because we are at extremes. Most people feel that if they can't hide, hoard, or save large amounts of money, they aren't wealthy. I'm sure you know that the economy is teaching us how to expand our consciousness. How? Instead of cutting down, or cutting back, we need to expand our consciousness to expect our every need to be fulfilled.

The Law of Abundance says, "Enough and to spare for your every need." Every time you say, "I am in lack," "I need," "I haven't got," "I can't find," or "I don't know," you have separated yourself from the reality of the truth of the Law of Abundance, which is in existence eternally.

Let me share with you how Robert and I observed the Law of Abundance in action.

In 1955, we were living in a new triplex in Hollywood. At the time, taxes and rents were increasing. Robert had lost his job at the restaurant, and I had a small, part-time job as a hand model on the *Bob Crosby Show*. Robert was collecting unemployment, and we were just able to make ends meet. Tenants all over town were receiving notices in their mailboxes that their rents had been raised, and we found a notice in our mailbox.

Robert said, "I don't want to open it. You open it."

The notice was from our landlady. "Dear Mr. and Mrs. Gaard, due to the raise in taxes, I am lowering your rent." I read it again, thinking she must have made a mistake. I knocked on her door and said, "Mrs. Rone, I think you've made a mistake. Don't you mean that you are raising our rent?"

She replied, "Oh, no, I meant what I wrote. I'm lowering your rent. You see, if I depended on your rent to cover all my expenses, I would really be in trouble, now, wouldn't I? I depend on the power of God to fulfill all my needs, not you."

I was dumbfounded.

Sensing my confusion, she said, "Don't worry about how it will be made up. He will take care of that."

Two weeks later, Mrs. Rone informed us that she had a new client. She was a vocal coach, and her new student was Mitzi Gaynor, the famous actress, singer, and dancer, who starred with Marilyn Monroe in *There's No Business Like Show Business*, *Anything Goes* with Bing Crosby and Donald O'Connor, and *The Joker Is Wild* alongside Frank Sinatra. Ms. Gaynor later won a Golden Globe as Best Actress for *South Pacific*. Mrs. Rone was the living example of the Law of Abundance in action. She was our first teacher along the path of enlightenment.

Dr. Bussell also talked about abundance.

> Express gratitude for everything you have. Give more of whatever you can, and then you will be in tune with the law and ready to receive without any necessary thought of return. Whenever there is an increase in the outflow, mentally and consciously accept an increase in your income. Put forth more energy in giving to bring this about. Working overtime in your job or giving of your talents, wherever they are needed, will eventually increase your income. If the motive is pure in giving, without any doubt or concern of receiving, you will reap the benefits. This is balance in the Universal Law.
>
> Giving and receiving is an eternal circle without beginning or end. If you don't give in comfortable ways, it will be taken in uncomfortable ways. Let me give you an example: A wealthy man who never gave to support a charity or any needy person, boasted of his wealth and that he never contributed to anything but his own business. Soon after, he complained to me that he had lost over a half million dollars from poor investments. He got back exactly what he gave.
>
> Thank God for whatever you need when you need it and it will be there.
>
> Are you wondering how you can give when you may not have anything to give, and when to begin to give? The answer is now! In any way you can. For instance, someone needs to be helped crossing the street, an unhappy person needs kind words and encouragement, someone who is incapacitated needs an errand, a deserving charity needs money,

but most of all, give your kind loving thoughts of peace, harmony, and love of God to the whole human race. This is where you begin. Then, you have given to your account in the Universal Bank. It will return with interest. What you put forth, regardless of what it may be, will return to you tenfold.

The only thing you're waiting for is yourself. You are waiting to get into the attitude of accepting the answer to your prayers. Enough and to spare is a definite law as much as the Law of Gravity, or the Law of Light, or Sound, or the Law of Thought. The Law of Abundance has never been repealed. It is as active today as it was in the beginning and is extending throughout creation. Therefore, it is without end. It is the law that has never failed in any sense at all—even in man's poor way of distribution, we have never in any way curtailed the Law of Abundance. There are still more than enough seeds in a watermelon.

Abundant supply doesn't entail accumulation. When you make that realization, you are a part of the great abundance. Whatever you do, remember to strike a balance. Realize an income commensurate with the energy that you spend. In other words, people who can help you and people whom you can help. "I and my abundance are one, enough and to spare for my every need." There is no break in the cycle.

The way to keep your abundance flowing is to be in harmony and in balance. This means you do not worship anything but the power that created it. Each person has his or her own abundance. You cannot take anyone's abundance from him or her. Each one has worked and earned his own by the good actions sent forth. So, you see, time or age cannot interfere with the law. Just because you don't receive what you want when you want it doesn't mean to retreat and say the law doesn't work. This is the time to look to yourself and recognize there is no flaw in the law. The flaw is within your thinking. It may be a lesson in steadfastness, patience, perseverance, or trust. Trust the law to know that your fulfillment is always at the right time.

It is also important for us to understand that you can't manipulate the law, or somewhere in your life you will be manipulated, which means you can't bargain with the power. For example, if you promise to do something in return for something that you have received through prayer, and you don't do it, you will have that same lesson returned to you. In other words, someone may promise to do something for you but neglect to fulfill the promise. This is how we learn our mistakes in applying the law through the experiences we live. It's a blessing that we live so many years. Sometimes it takes years to awaken and understand this magnificent law ever in operation for everyone's highest good, for the law is no respecter of persons; it just is. Many people use the law of giving and receiving merely for their own personal gain. This is a pitfall. Should you suddenly find yourself in a position where you have something stolen or lost, recognize that nothing is lost in the universe and know what is rightfully yours is returned to you. Every experience is an opportunity for introspection. Did you take from another in any way? Have you ever borrowed a book and failed to return it? Neglected to return money that was overpaid to you? This may sound like insignificant incidences, but not to the Universal Law. Nothing is omitted—good or bad. How well we hypnotize ourselves into believing we are not taking, but our conscience, which is our higher mind, never forgets.

Somewhere along the line, the scales must be balanced. Where we may have been wrong in the application of the law by our actions, we can always make it right through the correct application. We can always correct a mistake. Learn the lesson, and it will not repeat itself. The law, or God, whichever you choose to call it, is a loving one. Experiences will repeat themselves until you see the truth. Just like school—if you flunk a course, you take it over.

We have the example of people who are learning the responsibility of serving others, either elderly or handicapped relatives. If this responsibility is resented or given grudgingly, the lesson will last longer; however, if the attitude is seen as an opportunity to serve, the lesson will be shorn of much of its effect. Be grateful for what you are required to do; other lessons may be more difficult. You may not want your neighbor's lesson.

If the Law of Abundance only had to do with the money in the bank, it would be a very small and negative law, but it does have to do with all the things for which we have need—not just part of them, but all the things for which we have need.

Dr. Bussell gave us a very good example of the Law of Abundance in action. One Sunday morning, he related the need to buy the property next door to the church for an office and treatment rooms. He mentioned the amount needed and asked if anyone had an idea how we could raise the money. One hour later, he had all of the money needed. People came forth with pledges and checks. Escrow opened, and a month later, we purchased the adjoining house to fulfill the need. We learned the Universal Law of Abundance is enough and to spare for your every need.

A week after the lesson, a man came up to Dr. Bussell and said he was very disappointed. The Law of Abundance of enough and to spare didn't work in his life.

"I did as you told us, Doctor. I prayed for enough and to spare in the transaction." He pulled his hand out of his pocket, displayed a dime, and said, "All I have left is ten cents."

Dr. Bussell smiled and said, "That's your to spare." Dr. Bussell noticed that when we pray for things and work diligently for them, some of us receive small results. Perhaps that is what we expected! The greatest cause of unanswered prayer is the lack of large expectancy.

> If we will cultivate this principle in our lives, expecting large results, we'll find that those will be the results we'll get. There is only one thing that keeps our blessings from us ... it's our own consciousness. Our blessings can be big blessings, if we let them come in. We need to learn how to relax and let go without fear.
>
> Then, there is another group who have never reached the place where they have an abundance because they have in their consciousness the thought, "My parents lived in poverty, and their parents lived in poverty; therefore, abundance is not for me." There are millions of people who have that excuse, and until they can raise their consciousness to a place

where they can realize the law is "no respecter of persons," they will live in the "less than enough" all of their lives as their ancestors may have done.

Everything we can bring into consciousness, we can have. The law is definite. Be careful of what you ask for. You may not want it later.

There is a fine point I would like you to understand about the law. If it's money you work for to purchase something you want, the money could be needed for other purposes: for bills or unexpected emergencies. If you hold the thought of what you need in consciousness, the money will come to pay for it. Money is the law (energy) in action. It's not meant to be worshipped. If you worship money, money will be your teacher. When people place money before the law, they will perish by it. There have been many people down through history who have become billionaires and have wasted away the money. If all they thought about was money, they could lose their family, their health, and their empires.

Henry Ford said, "I spent my health to get my wealth, and now I'm spending my wealth to get my health."

Don't try to judge another person's life or the way they are living. The Law of Life is not through with them yet. Be concerned with what you are doing; you are only responsible for yourself. You do it right! You reap the benefits of living the law, and you won't have to worry about anyone else.

Let's move to the area of writing checks and paying bills. It seems that every day we are all inundated with bills. What is your first reaction? A sinking feeling and *Oh, no not again!* It seems when we have just finished paying all our bills, here they come again, and our first reaction might be resentment and fear. If we want to live a more expanding, abundant life, this is the place to change our attitudes.

Stay in an attitude of gratitude for a continuous flow of abundance that fulfills your every need now. When you are steadfast in knowing the law will supply your need, you will never be without. As you are mentally directed to do all you can do to create your abundance, the law moves with you. Your desire and thoughts magnetize this to you. Recognize and be aware that the Universal Law is helping you. You are never alone. Knowing and expressing true gratitude for a continuous flow of abundance will expand your prosperity.

Another helpful suggestion is to write "thank you" on every check you receive before you cash it. This not only helps you, but also those who see it. Without question, gratitude opens the door to abundance.

Someone asked me the other day about borrowing money. If you could understand that everything you say and do sets up a pattern to recycle into your life, you would be more careful about the seeds you plant. If you truly know and believe in a power greater than you are to fulfill your every need at the time you need it, you may never have to borrow a cent. There are, of course, exceptions—like buying a house. The danger of borrowing money means that, within the consciousness, there is a negative thought that says, "If I don't have enough, I can always borrow." This sets up a negative pattern to recycle again. Once these habit patterns have been repeated, they are difficult to change. If you are truly in the consciousness of the Law of Abundance, you will never need to borrow money.

How about loaning money, especially to a friend? Many good friendships have been terminated because of money issues. If the loan isn't repaid soon—very soon—there will be an attitude of resentment on the part of the lender, and a feeling of guilt in the borrower. This will produce an estrangement in the relationship. If you feel the necessity to loan money to a dear friend because at the time it is crucial to him, give what you can without any thought of return. This way, there is no resentment on your part, and if it is returned, you will be gratefully surprised. This also preserves the friendship. Chances are if the money is not returned, the person would avoid you and be too embarrassed to ask for more. If you continued to loan money, the person would never learn to expect or depend on the law that provides their own abundance.

If children were taught the Law of Abundance from childhood, they would take responsibility for their abundance. They would know their purpose and reason for being here and develop the talent they have within. We all have more than one talent. When one door closes, another one opens, better than before. There is always room at the top for new ideas and inventions to come into expression where you can be a success.

New and original ideas are always in Universal Mind, if you take the time to meditate. If you ask to

be of service utilizing all the talents that you have
been given for the good of all, you will have become
a part of the Universal Law of Abundance.

When I first began teaching these principles I learned from Dr.
Bussell, one particular example of the law as seen in action comes
to mind. I was single at the time and supporting myself and
very much in need of $500 to pay my bills. I meditated and
thanked God for my need fulfilled. That evening after class,
when I counted the donations, among them were five hundred-
dollar bills. I wanted to thank the person, so I mentally reviewed
the people who had attended that evening and called the man I
assumed left the donation. After I verified that he was responsible
for leaving the money, I said, "Thank you so much, but why did
you leave five hundred dollars?"

To this he replied, "Well, I was so grateful for what I have
learned and how much I have received; I wanted to express my
gratitude. Meditatively, I asked the amount I should leave. My
direction was to leave five hundred dollars."

A perfect example of being in the right place at the right time
surfaced when Mr. Bud Scully, retired president of Financial
Guaranty Insurance Brokers, Inc. met one of the students from
my class and the conversation turned to the Essene teachings.

Bud was at a low point in his life after going through a
divorce. He joined AA, and he was looking for a way to rebuild
his life. He had been a salesman for many years, but he was now
starting a new business with two partners, a small bank line of
credit, and a high degree of nervousness and fear.

Bud's lesson was to shift his consciousness from salesman
to chairman of a corporation before his position could change
and manifest. He had to think and speak as a top executive.
Otherwise, he would have stayed in the same position as a

salesman. "What made me succeed were two words I was taught: gratitude and joy," Bud said.

He is in his eighties, and he awakens every morning at 5:45, exercises at the gym for about an hour—which puts him in a good, positive attitude—and then goes to work. "I don't meditate, per se. I just keep in the positive meditation all day. It's very easy to be positive when you have the answers and are on the right track."

Always remember that you have the power to change things. Your mind is your greatest asset. You are never alone; there is a Universal Law that responds to your every thought. So watch what you think! If you don't want what you are thinking, be wise and *don't think it*!

Our lesson is to accept more of the eternal abundance that has been here since the beginning of time. How? By believing, expecting, trusting, and accepting all with gratitude. Look around in the universe. It is filled and overflowing with abundance and continues to give daily. Accept your inheritance and eliminate the pain.

If you find yourself unemployed, you may be able to do now what you have always wanted to do, but have never had the time. Take time to be silent and meditate on your real purpose—what you came to do. Patience and expectation will bring your reward.

If you desire something you do not really need, you may be sorry you desired this. Ask yourself if you really need it. Ask in faith believing, and the law or God will always fulfill your need. Remember the three questions:

1: Is it good for me? (Always checking yourself first)
2: Is it good for the other person or persons?
3: Does it hurt anyone?

If the answers pass all the tests, then you are right to ask the universe for your desire.

CHAPTER 9

Removing Pain

To me, one of the most memorable incidents of how pain was eliminated took place in Hollywood four doors away from the church. The incident taught me the stupendous power contained within the true state of Peace.

Early one morning, an accident occurred during the construction of a new apartment building, directly across the street from Dr. Bussell's residence. A workman's chainsaw slipped and nearly severed his leg just below the knee. After the construction crew called for an ambulance, one workman ran to nearby apartments to find someone who could administer emergency help. He noticed Dr. Bussell's nameplate on the door of his apartment. He ran to inform the other workmen that there was a doctor across the street. Anxious and in desperation, they carried the man to Dr. Bussell's door and rang the bell.

When Dr. Bussell opened the door, he encountered several men begging for his help. It was obvious the injured man was experiencing excruciating pain and bleeding profusely. Dr. Bussell knelt down and placed both of his hands on the workman's injured leg. In a few short moments, the man closed his eyes and completely relaxed. everyone present thought he was unconscious. Meanwhile, the ambulance arrived and transported the injured man to the emergency room at the nearest hospital.

Shortly thereafter, Dr. Bussell received a phone call from a doctor at the hospital.

"Is this Dr. Bussell?"

"Yes, it is," he replied.

"I am the attending physician at the community hospital. There are workmen here who related that you recently assisted a man whose leg was nearly amputated. Is this true?"

"Yes, that's true."

"I need to ask you what anesthetic you administered or what medication you gave this man because he is still unconscious."

"I gave him nothing," said Dr. Bussell

"But you must have given him something; only a doctor would know how to put an injured man to sleep who is in this type of acute condition."

In a very understanding and kind voice Dr. Bussell answered, "I am a minister, not a medical doctor. I merely let the peace of God fill him, and from the realization of this complete peace, he fell asleep and there was no pain."

The physician was baffled and at a loss for words.

This may seem like an extraordinary story about how Dr. Bussell was able to go into that quiet place to fill this man's body with peace, sparing him excruciating pain. This incident proved that relaxation and peace play a key part in eliminating pain. Dr. Bussell could only do this by being in a complete state of peace himself. He often said, "We must get into the peace that passeth all understanding before we can help anyone."

A good example of correctly coping with accidents and pain presented itself when Don, one of the students in class, came in one evening with his arm wrapped from the wrist to the elbow.

I asked him what happened, and he smiled and said, "Nothing much. A waitress spilled scalding coffee on my arm, but I refused to accept the pain. Just as I learned in class with my exhale breath, I kept saying, 'I am free of pain, I am free from pain. I release and let go of any pain and the peace of God fills me now and I am one with peace,' and it worked!"

If you look deep within yourself, you will find pain is your teacher on every level—mental, physical, and spiritual. Pain will force you to find the truth and learn what you need to learn to set you free.

The greatest blessing is being able to tune in and ask your Higher Self, "What am I to learn from this experience? Reveal the truth to me." When the lesson has been learned, the pain will most likely disappear. This is true of all body ailments.

To be in the attitude of peace, Dr. Bussell taught me that the first thing we need to do is relax. Sitting quietly, removing all thoughts but the thought of "relax," we can begin to let go of tension or stress. In taking long, deep breaths, we will put the mind and body in a state of quiet peace, and every cell and muscle begins to relax.

First, place your right hand over the area of pain, because the right hand is the "giving" side of our body. The left hand receives the energy, and the right hand gives the energy. In other words, the left hand pulls out pain, and the right hand puts in peace. In using both hands, you are putting your body in peace and relaxation. Then, you can repeat this statement, "I relax and let go of anything that prevents me from my perfect peace and relaxation, and in this state, it allows me to be free from pain."

I remember a very loving elderly couple who sat in front of me at Dr. Bussell's weekly classes. I noticed them for several years. They were always so happy together. One week they were absent, and I heard the husband had passed away. The following week, the wife came in, smiling and happy. We couldn't understand how she could be so happy. She explained that she was so grateful for the many years they had together, and there was no reason for her to be sad. She turned her feeling of loss into one of gratitude.

Pain in loss is more in the mind than the body, but it can be transferred to the body if the mind cannot change. Helping another person who has a heavier lesson and harder life can relieve some of our own pain. Expressing gratitude every day for the smallest things in your life will relieve more pain.

Our disappointments or frustrations are due to relinquishing control. If someone isn't doing what we want them to do we feel—frustration! Or if something didn't turn out the way we wanted it to—disappointment! Since the Divine Presence created, maintains, and sustains, we might as well give it up to the Power that Knows All, and be at peace.

In having this attitude, the experience will be shorn of much effect on you. "It's not what happens to you that counts; it's your reaction to what happens that counts."

In order to become illumined and self-mastered, there are attributes of God that we carve in the diamond of our souls.

- Love
- Kindness
- Gentleness
- Humility
- Trust
- Generosity
- Patience
- Steadfastness
- Order
- Justice
- Cleanliness
- Truth

In every experience of emotional pain, you are becoming more loving, kind, gentle, etc., so that light will shine through and you will not only walk in light, you will *be* the light.

CHAPTER 10

Your Harmony Tone

In one of his lectures, Dr. Bussell said, "I wonder how many of you are aware of possessing a harmony tone that completely changes the vibration of the body and situations in your life?"

Dr. Bussell then introduced us to the Harmony Tone exercise. This starts by identifying your Harmony Center, which is located between the seventh cervical vertebra and the first dorsal vertebra. The practice of distributing the harmony tone, from the Harmony Center throughout the body, is effective for all conditions at all times. I found that I could even overcome a cold on the very first day by practicing the harmony exercise every hour on the hour.

Several articles have been written about harmony, but the first recognition of the existence of the Harmony Center within the human body was found in the early Dravidian writings from more than 3,500 years ago. The Dravidian language was native to Southern India, which was based on Sanskrit, the oldest language in the world. The Dravidian writings explained where the Harmony Tone was located in the body. The Essenes used the harmony exercise every morning as a daily practice, and Dr. Bussell incorporated the harmony exercise in the daily meditation to set our bodies and lives in harmony. Through time, the spiritual practices based on this knowledge were lost in antiquity, and the rediscovery of the harmony exercise is one of our greatest blessings.

Dr. Bussell said, "The greatest healing agent in the world is harmony. Health is harmony, and harmony is bringing all things into order. In the Bible, the establishment of harmony is referred to in Genesis chapter 1 and 2." "In the beginning God created the heavens and the earth".

Entire two chapters of the beginning of Creation is set in Harmony.

The awareness of the presence of harmony is developed through observation. You can easily observe harmony in nature. You will see it in the trees, the flowers, and all life everywhere. In one of Dr. Bussell's classes he shared with us how he used the harmony exercise.

> Every morning when I am preparing Mrs. Bussell's breakfast in the kitchen, I mentally do the harmony exercise while standing in front of the window by the sink. I noticed four little animals outside the kitchen window gathered together a few feet apart to partake of the harmony: a blue jay, a cat, a squirrel, and a rabbit. The cat licked his paw, the bird was picking the ground, the squirrel was crunching some food, and the rabbit hopped around. None of them were interfering with each other's space or privacy. They merely gathered every morning when I came in the kitchen in harmony.

The planets in space also follow an orderly course at regular times in perfect harmony, and they make beautiful music. Pythagoras, the Greek philosopher and scientist who lived in the fifth century

BC, proposed a theory known as the harmony of the spheres, also referred to as music of the spheres and universal harmony. Pythagoras believed that the sun, moon, and planets emit a unique hum or orbital resonance based on their orbital revolution, and that the quality of life on earth reflects the tenor of celestial sounds, which are physically imperceptible to the human ear.

Harmony is order. You cannot have order without harmony or harmony without order. Your own expression of harmony is in and around you wherever you are: in the clothes you wear, the car you drive, the space you occupy at work, and the place where you live. If you are not comfortable when you return home, look to your level of harmony within. You can reestablish harmony wherever you are by doing your harmony exercise.

Years after Dr. Bussell passed away, nineteen-year-old Richard Wagner came to my class. He was lost and confused, but he was so anxious to learn that he moved from his parents' home to an apartment near the classroom.

Richard had just returned from New York, where he struggled to be an actor. He was a college dropout, but he studied philosophy and transcendental meditation. He also read every book by Alan Watts, best known as an interpreter of Zen Buddhism. Richard was obviously looking for something, but he didn't know how to put everything he was learning in perspective.

Although Richard was raised Jewish, he found harmony and a common ground of all religions through the teaching and philosophy of the Essenes. "I didn't realize thoughts are things," Richard said. "I hadn't approached that before—that you are what you think. This became my way of life."

Richard used his creative mind to design jewelry and start his own successful business. After many years, the universe tested Richard, when a fire wiped out the building and his business. Richard never lost his harmony, and through meditation and the harmony exercises, he was able to reinvent himself. Richard has a loving wife and three wonderful sons, and he resides in Beverly Hills.

You will find that the harmony exercise is one of the most important lessons and exercises in life. We are a part of the harmony that was first established. In relationship to our body, we must realize that our body is the temple of God and the spirit dwells within us. Knowing this, we can comprehend the importance of keeping ourselves in better condition—physically, mentally, and spiritually—because it is our duty to keep this temple in the very best possible condition that we can.

For instance, when the soul attaches itself to your body and you take your first breath, your harmony tone is established, and it remains with you for the rest of your life. Every nerve, gland, and organ vibrates. When one of the organs is out of harmony, it is no longer vibrating at its natural rate of frequency. It may be slow and need to be raised, or too fast and need to be lowered to the normal rate. This is where your harmony exercise plays a very important part in your life. When you do your harmony exercise, every single one of your organs is brought to its normal rate of vibration, and the body is brought back in tune. You can correct an ailment or prevent a disease. The name of the disease doesn't matter; what matters is that you recognize the Higher Power that creates only good.

Dr. Bussell guided us through the Harmony Tone exercise, as follows.

> If we were tuning the violin, we would ask the pianist to strike the E note, and then we would tune the rest of the violin to that E string. We might consider that the harmony center of the human body was like the E string of the violin. We must tune our entire body to that particular note.

A Way of Life

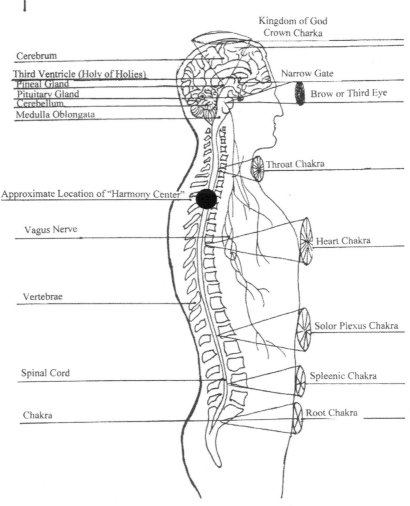

Harmony Tone Center (Diagram)

When you first begin your exercise, you don't notice the illumination, but as you start down your left arm, it's like a neon tube. The whole tube lights up. When you think to your harmony center, you automatically pick up your tone with your mind and if I say, "Carry the thought to the top of your head," you couldn't do anything else because that's the way your mind works. From that point, you can direct your thought down the left side of your head and down your left arm. This is when the light begins to travel. When the tone and the light travel down the arm, it moves rapidly and extends to the fingers of the left hand. That remains light. It is very important that you leave the harmony tone in the palm of your left hand.

When you go back to the harmony center and again pick up the tone, you go to the top of the head again. It does not show any particular gleam of light until you start down again. This time, you will carry the tone along the left side of the neck. At the center of the neck, there is a large nerve that divides: one part of it goes out over the arm, and the other part goes down the leg. Now we follow the one that goes down to the leg, through the shoulder, through the torso, out over the hip, down to the foot, the toes of the foot, and again we leave the tone there. We followed the great nerve trunk, the largest nerve trunk in the body.

It's the one that supplies all the nervous energy, the motor energy, and the sensory energy to the leg. There are little nerves and nervelets that lead to all the cells of your body, and just the instant that harmony is set up in the leg, at that very instant, you begin to build up a harmony in your body because the small nerve and nervelets are carrying to every cell of the body that particular harmony until every nerve and every cell is perfectly harmonized. The left side of your body is now illuminated.

Then you start down the right side and establish a line of light down the right side. After you carry the tone down the right side of the head, arm, and hand, the color will have reached and spread down the right leg, foot, and toes. The last time, carry the tone to the top of the head, and go down the spinal column vertebra by vertebra along through the torso, directly through the harmony center, past the small of the back, and down to the very tip of the spine.

There are seven ganglions along the spine. All of them are nerve centers, and we touch every nerve center in the body. In fact, every nerve root in the body carries to every cell that perfect harmony. Then, from the tip of the spine, we come up on the front of the body, the pelvic region, abdomen, chest, lungs, throat, cavities of the face, and on to the top of the head where we end.

In this exercise, we have traversed every nerve trunk in the body and every nerve center, so every tiny nervelet in your body is reached and harmonized, including the cells of the hairs of your head. Every part of you will be in harmony. If you are interrupted in the midst of doing this exercise, begin again so that you will have complete balanced harmony in your body without any break. Be sure you do not do this automatically without thinking. We need to think vigorously in order to become illumined.

It is so necessary for us to have harmony, and if it weren't useful and beneficial, I'm sure that we wouldn't have been endowed with this great Harmony Center. The animal kingdom doesn't have it. There is nothing in creation that I know of that has the Harmony Center that we have.

Many people doing the harmony exercise have transformed angry situations into peace and harmony. Estranged relationships have been mended, broken friendships repaired, and families brought together in love—all from the astounding effects of using and sharing this exercise.

The same principle can be applied to any situation with which you are confronted, and the outcome will always have the same result: *for the good of all.* Our world and all the people in it can benefit with more universal harmony. When we place ourselves in harmony with all humanity, and care enough, we will have peace, happiness, and universal harmony for all.

CHAPTER 11

Law of Right Action

We all want our lives to be in perfect Right Action, but do we know the meaning of Right Action? The Universal Law is clear and simple. It merely means "God's love in motion."

To be more specific, it means that you are in the right place at the right time with the right people, saying and doing all the right things. Everyone desires this. There is a word that exemplifies Right Action. You've heard it used many times. The word is righteousness (right-use-ness). Right Action is being consistent with the Divine Plan—the perfect plan for your life. We come with a perfect plan, and if you have been seeking the truth for a long time, you might be able to find it. If you are ready, the universe automatically provides a way for you to be in the right place at the right time. All you need to do is be alert, watch for the signs, and take action.

Dr. Bussell's life was consistent with Right Action. He had so much insight that he always intuitively knew when, how, and where to locate the student or students who were ready to advance spiritually. He would feel the vibrations of a location and *know* that this was where a little "note from the universe" would help the seeking student find his or her teacher.

Dr. Bussell asked Mrs. Kettle, a very influential woman and student of Chirothesia, to move to Manhattan Beach and place an ad in the *Sea Breeze*, a local paper for the beach community, about the spiritual development classes being offered. Mrs. Kettle was also instrumental in introducing Ernest Holmes, founder of Religious Science, to Dr. Bussell where he received counsel and healing treatments.

One person, Mrs. Ewing responded to the classes, but she did not follow through in actually attending Dr. Bussell's classes. Her husband, a Harvard graduate, was skeptical and not interested in seeking any kind of "spiritual" help from anybody in Hollywood.

Two years later, they had a son born with serious digestive problems. This touched their hearts, and the Ewings searched everywhere for a cure. Mrs. Ewing's neighbor referred her to Dr. Bussell for healing treatments. This came as a surprise to Mrs. Ewing because her family no longer lived in Manhattan Beach (where she had read the ad). They had moved thirty miles away to Whittier, California. She wondered how her neighbor knew of Dr. Bussell. Although it felt like a sign or "the right action" to follow, it wasn't until four years later that Mrs. Ewing contacted Dr. Bussell. She came across another ad for Dr. Bussell's classes— this time in her Whittier local paper. Mr. Ewing, who had experienced so much suffering over his son's condition, finally agreed with his wife to see Dr. Bussell.

Mr. and Mrs. Ewing arrived at Dr. Bussell's at eleven o'clock for their scheduled appointment. Dr. Bussell looked at his watch.

"You're late."

"No, we're right on time," Mrs. Ewing said.

Dr. Bussell focused his sparkling eyes on the couple, indicating a playful heart, and repeated, "No, you're late."

The Ewings got the message. It was obvious to them that they should have arrived five years earlier.

Their story is a perfect example of how opportunity presents itself when at least one person is ready to hear the truth. As you probably know, "all of the flowers in the garden do not bloom at the same time." Mrs. Ewing was ready to learn more when she first read the ad in the newspaper, but Mr. Ewing had to reach a place of suffering and endure it for a while before he could be receptive to any help. This was his lesson. When we are partners with someone, we take on their lessons and they take on ours. It's mutually accepted when we come together. Mrs. Ewing waited until her husband was ready, and they grew together.

Their arrival and receptivity was all that was necessary. Their son's illness was cured after several healing treatments with Dr. Bussell, and the Ewings became loyal students to the newly found spiritual path. Mrs. Ewing and I have remained great friends ever since.

There is no set time for Right Action. The teacher waits because time is the enfolding of God's plan, and it's always perfect. If you program yourself to always be in the right place at the right time with the right people, you will be.

I think we all have a tendency to prevent Right Action from taking place in our lives by being impatient. We spend a lot of time asking, "Why isn't it happening now?"

Are you aware that the amount of time it takes for enfoldment and manifestation is up to you? Ask yourself the following:

1. How long do you think it's going to take?
2. What lesson do you have to learn?
3. What do you think you have to do before the manifestation takes place?

All of us have had someone removed from our lives that we revered, loved, and depended upon. The day came for me when

Dr. Bussell left us in physical form. After his transition, I felt the loss for a long time. However, I always kept his example silently resting in my heart. I realized this had to happen so we would all find our own inner power and security.

In 1967, five years after Dr. Bussell made the transition, I put my own life in Right Action and meditatively asked if I was meant to teach what I had learned. Since it was Right Action and the response was yes, I mentally asked to be given a sign. Seven people in seven days wanted me to share the wisdom of the Law of God.

The very next day, while waiting for my daughter to exit the school, another mother and I started talking, as mothers do, while waiting for our children. Sherry, a Beverly Hills socialite, was fascinated with Chirothesia and the Law of God. She asked me many questions, and then she asked if I would be willing to teach her.

The following day, as I took Greta to Summer Bible School, a woman named Sheila approached me. Her daughter was another one of Greta's classmates. Sheila had heard about the teachings and asked if I would teach her as well.

The day after that as I visited my doctor's office, his assistant started asking me questions about the Law of God. She also heard about Chirothesia and the teachings and was curious to learn more.

A day later, as I was having my hair done, the beautician was so enthralled by what I told her about Chirothesia that she closed the beauty salon and came to my home so I could teach her more.

By the end of the week—within seven days—seven people, all strangers, suddenly crossed my path. They all approached me and asked if I would teach them the Law of God. I had my sign. I built an extension to my home, which became a chapel, and I taught for the next thirty years.

One of the original seven, Sherry Shelley, who through her dedication, loyalty, and support of the Footlighters Child Life Center for Abused and Handicapped Children, was chosen "Woman of the Year" in 2000.

Sherry had the opportunity to put the Law of Right Action to use when her husband was diagnosed with Alzheimer's disease. Sherry repeated to herself, "All right, God, it's my turn to take over my life and knowing with God all things are possible, I can handle anything." She and her husband had an airplane parts company, and Sherry knew nothing about the business. She sat in her bedroom and used her overstuffed ottoman for a desk. She started by calling all over the world and asking for the top executives. She explained her husband's condition and how, despite her lack of knowledge of his business, she had taken over. She was quick to stress that she was a very fast learner. Top executives, who rarely offered help, took the time to educate Sherry. Sherry asked for help, and she received it. She was not afraid. The opposite of fear is faith, and that's how she lived. She was so busy that she didn't have time to count her money.

Years later, Sherry had several tragedies befall her. She found love again, only to lose him to cancer. Her only daughter, who had been ill for some time, also died of cancer on her birthday. Sherry, too, had breast and colon cancer.

No one can understand how she went through these losses and survived with the happy, positive outlook she had. Sherry said, "It's easy when you know the truth and even better when you know everything is in perfect Right Action. I never asked why because I knew God had a perfect plan, and I accepted that."

Sherry's spiritual strength and soul desire to be an example to others proved the Law of Right Action in the Divine Plan. We are never given more than we can withstand. When you meditate and discover the answers, the problems are not as difficult.

As a spiritual teacher, my greatest happiness was watching the transformation take place in the lives of the students who daily applied the laws to every situation.

Another student, William Wiles of Newport Beach, was quite depressed when he came to class. He had lost a ten-year corporate job, and his marriage had come to an end. He was searching for something that would bring him through this turmoil and agony. He had two sons, six and four, who were his primary responsibility. From his understanding of the Universal Law, William chose not to become involved with any woman until his sons were grown. He raised them through their teenage years and into college. Having faith in Right Action, he believed the right woman would appear at the right time … and she did.

William's greatest test, however, which made him use everything he had learned, came when he learned that his twenty-year-old son had been killed in an auto accident. His son had just finished his first year in college. If William hadn't learned about the Universal Laws, he might not have made it through this tragedy.

"I knew I was surrounded in peace," explained William. "My strength came from knowing life is eternal and there is no separation. I realized the need for people to learn the Universal Laws. I conferred with Dr. Gaard and became a minister of the teaching. I learned the most important lesson of my life—faith." For many years, William was a partner at Lyon Studios, a successful commercial film company.

In 1998, I was approached by Lisa, a student who wanted me to hear her boyfriend sing. She said John Kimberling had a very unusual operatic voice, and she was convinced that everyone would love to hear him. I wasn't interested in opera singers, but I agreed to listen to John anyway. I was absolutely spellbound. I wasn't the only one who felt the soul connection when he sang.

John had given up singing before he met Lisa in acting school, but when she heard him sing, she encouraged him to share his gift. After following the teachings of the Universal Laws, doors suddenly opened for singing engagements. In 2000, John was accepted into the Los Angeles Opera. When John heard that a famous writer of Broadway musicals was searching for a tenor to fill the role in a new production to open in Santa Barbara, John meditated. It worked, and he was called to audition.

"Needless to say, I was nervous," John said. "But before I finished singing the score, I was interrupted." More than a thousand singers had auditioned for this role, but John was the one who received the part!

John's lesson was patience and confidence, knowing there is a right time and right place for everything in a divine plan. If you want your life to be better, the best and wisest thing you can possibly do is place your trust in the Law of Right Action.

CHAPTER 12

The Law of Protection

Did you know there is a way to be protected wherever you are? And in the same manner you can protect others as well? Would you believe that it's a gift you already possess?

I had no idea that this knowledge was going to save me from serious injury when I used it just two days after I learned the lesson. There is indeed something else we can do besides locks for protection and alarms on our property for precaution. If you are ready to utilize this gift, you will surely benefit by becoming familiar with additional material on the subject of protection.

Dr. Bussell's shares the following lesson:

> It's the little-known Auric Shield, sometimes referred to as the Ring Pass Not or the Ring of Love. It doesn't matter by what name we call it; it's a very definite material substance, which is a natural gift. This natural gift can be developed and brought entirely under your control. You will find the shield mentioned in the Bible. Interpreting the passage, Ephesians 6:11, "Put on the whole armor of God, that you may be able to stand against the wiles of

the devil." The armor is the shield that protects you. When you use the Auric Shield, you are protected from accidents, onslaughts, people, places, or things that may be harmful to you.

The aura, which is a natural emanation all around you, extends from two inches to several feet at right angles from your body. It's more or less involuntary and emotional. The emanation is a smoky gray color composed of millions of tiny strands of vaporous material resembling fog, and indicates a very high vibration. In cases of fear or great alarm, the shield appears to be more evident. When you consciously call this into action, it takes on a very different appearance. If you are not conscious of the development of the Auric Shield, its radius extends just a few inches. However, if you have been exposed to danger, you will sense an unusual development, and with proper practice, you can extend it a great distance, sometimes as much as several feet. Have you ever noticed the hair rise on a cat's back, or even on a dog's, especially when they are afraid and want to protect themselves? Did you ever feel the hair rise on your head or arms? This is the same principle. Then you understand the function of the Auric Shield. The more you know and use your natural gifts, the greater and stronger your protection. For example, glass is a barrier to the movement of air, but not to sunlight. The shield shuts out the lower or negative vibrations and seems to allow the higher ones to penetrate, like coming through glass.

If you were to attend the symphony encased in the Auric Shield, you would hear and enjoy the music more. The conscious awareness of the shield will also protect you from emotions while viewing violent scenes in movies or television. The more you remind yourself to consciously extend your own vibration of protection, the longer it will last. An advanced student, who consistently practices the use of the Auric Shield, can be protected in all manners of so-called contagious diseases, where there is no membranous contact.

Shortly after I learned this lesson in 1955, I was involved in a serious car accident. It occurred when I was driving on San Vicente Boulevard in Los Angeles. The boulevard was under construction and full of machinery and equipment. All of a sudden, a skip loader emerged from between the other machinery. There were no guards or cones to provide any warning. The shovel of the skip loader crushed the left front of my car, right up to the door. I slammed on the brakes, but the force of the action threw my right foot off the brake and onto the accelerator. The car went out of control, jumped the curb, and headed for a spiked tractor roller in the center of the boulevard.

At the onset of the accident, I immediately remembered to use the Auric Shield, and I said, "God is; I am divinely protected now." At that instant, even though I was being tossed back and forth, since cars had no seatbelts at that time, I felt as if I had been immersed in thick cotton. I put both hands at the top of the steering wheel to protect my head from going through the windshield. When the workmen rushed to pry the car door open, they said, "My God, lady, are you all right?"

I hesitated, saying, "I think so."

They carefully escorted me out of the car to a temporary office trailer, and I phoned Robert. When Robert arrived and saw the car, he couldn't believe I wasn't hurt. I may have been in shock, but I was extremely grateful that I escaped any serious injuries. I relayed the incident to Dr. Bussell during our next class.

As usual, he smiled and said, "Well, you found out the Auric Shield works, didn't you?"

"Yes, I did," I said, in a very convincing tone.

Years later, I taught the Auric Shield lesson, and I later learned that one of the men in class used it one night as he drove home. On the freeway, a car in the far lane went out of control and headed toward him. He mentally pulled up the Auric Shield, surrounding himself and his car in protection. The car coming toward him suddenly veered off to the right, and he was never touched. He shared this story with great relief and gratitude.

Another time, the young actress, Stepfanie Kramer, best known for playing Detective Dee Dee McCall on the TV series *Hunter* came to see me.

"I was especially drawn to Beverly. I felt strongly that I needed to connect with her and to know her," Stepfanie said.

The Universal Laws resonated with what Stepfanie was reading and studying at the time. She has now been practicing the laws for the last twenty-five years, which brought her to a higher level of consciousness and awareness within herself. It has completely changed her life in a profound way and has become second nature to her mind and being.

> I don't have to think about it. It's just there. There have been many occasions when I have been able to put the teaching into effect to have a positive outcome occur. For example, I was with my brother and his wife in West Hollywood. We were returning from a show at night, walking to my car. I had just opened the door and sat inside. My brother was getting in the front

seat and his wife in the back, when out of nowhere came two masked men with guns. One of the men held a large gun directly into my brother's chest. They started yelling for our wallets, watches, and purses. Immediately in my mind, and without hesitation, I went into the teaching and said, "God is; I am divinely protected now in every way with my Auric Shield." I visualized it surrounding myself, my brother, his wife, and the car. I kept focusing that energy as I handed over my purse. I calmed down my sister-in-law, and I mentally extended the energy to my brother so that he would not be shot. I was wearing a lot of valuable jewelry that night, which the gunmen didn't even see. My brother gave them his watch and wallet, while my sister-in-law handed over her purse and jewelry. I gave them my purse, yet it was as if they didn't see me. They spoke only to my brother and his wife. When the gunmen left, I ran for help. The police quickly arrived, and we later dealt with the inconvenience of changing the locks on my home, but thankfully we were unharmed. I had completely focused on God's light and the Auric Shield surrounding us with divine protection at that critical moment, especially for my brother, and it worked! The next morning, at seven, I received a call that my purse had been found. Everything was exactly how I had left it. Nothing had been removed except for the cash. My credit cards, driver's license, and checkbook were all there.

We can use the Auric Shield mentally or physically. Stepfanie immediately changed levels of consciousness and realized the power of the Auric Shield's protective light. It completely surrounded her, similar to bulletproof glass, and she mentally extended this light to encompass her brother and sister-in-law. Life will always provide the experience to prove what you have learned. Knowledge is power. Knowledge without application is useless. Be sure to use it.

Dr. Bussell learned the use of the Auric Shield when he studied in India.

A pit was dug eight feet square and eight feet deep. A few stones were thrown into the pit and then filled with cedar logs, which were fired. After they had been entirely consumed and nothing was left but a white ash and a few charred embers, while the heat was yet so intense that we ordinary mortals could not approach nearer than sixty or seventy feet from the pit, our teacher clad in very light raiment stepped into this pit. While the temperature was near the boiling point, or possibly above, he remained there for thirty minutes, during which time he gave us the lesson on the Auric Shield.

When he came forth, there were no visible indications of any nature that would suggest that he had been in an abnormal temperature or was in any way agitated or confused by the experience. No parts of his clothing were seared or burned. Even the flesh of his back and limbs were as cool, or cooler than those of the spectators who were quite well satisfied to remain at least one hundred feet from the speaker's stand while he delivered the lesson. Most of the students saw very plainly the development of the Auric Shield. This preparation required but a few moments, and it was soon relaxed after the teacher came forth from the seething cauldron. Some people have the idea that there is something superhuman in connection with the use of a natural protection. If you believe that these things are not consistent with the enlightened consciousness today, you may have many shocks and surprises.

In the moments of impending danger to yourself, always remember to follow the prescribed procedure. There is a lot of power in the Auric Shield when you know how it works, and you are able to use it. Use it every day before you leave the house. Surround your home in the protective light of the Auric Shield. Use it the moment you get into your car and as you drive up and down the streets and highways. Surround your car with the Auric Shield, and watch the other cars move away, as if they are making room especially for you. Never use it as a plaything. We don't test the law. In other words, if you choose to go through a red light, don't think you are being protected. We must obey the physical man-made laws as well as the spiritual laws. Remember that there are countless ways, many opportunities, and so many times when you can use the Auric Shield to your advantage. The shield can only be used for good.

If you are ever in a relationship where the person is angry and the anger is directed toward you, remain in a state of calm and pull up your Auric Shield. You will not become a part of the emotion of anger, which resolves nothing.

Here is the secret of the Auric Shield:

First: Release and let go of any thoughts in your mind. Center yourself and hold steady. Don't allow too many thoughts to distract your attention. Eliminate all emotion. Be calm and quiet.

Second: Realize and visualize your Auric Shield extending at right angles from your entire body, the same as fog. (Perhaps when you were a child, you might have noticed how you can move fog with your hands. It's the same principle.) As you realize and visualize your Auric Shield extending at right angles from your entire body, you might notice a slight tingling sensation passing over your body, especially along your limbs. You will obtain the best results providing you're in a meditative state with your eyes closed. With further knowledge and acquaintance of its existence, you can pull it up in a split-second, if necessary. Then you become so familiar with it that the mere thought of Auric Shield will immediately manifest itself.

Third: Your thought of protection will enhance its activity. Remember not to allow the thoughts of fear or anger. The Auric Shield does not protect when one is in a negative state of emotion. As you mentally extend your thought of protection, you will extend the shield. Be consciously aware of the solar plexus area. Even after you have extended the shield, invariably there will be an open space over the stomach, for this is your most sensitive part. This is where you take in all of your emotions and negative feelings from other people. Sometimes it may even result in having a stomachache. This part of your body requires special attention. You will need to cover this area doubly. It would be a good idea to take your hands and pull it up as if you were drawing material covering this part of your body. The Auric Shield seems to start at the lower part of the body, as if it were a shroud to be drawn up from the feet, encasing the entire body. Make sure that it's closed over the top of your head. If you are a beginner, this envelope will remain for approximately five to ten minutes, and if it's necessary, repeat this exercise. You can use your hands or your thoughts. In the beginning, you might want to use your hands and feel this as you move from your feet up over your body—over the top of your head. If you have continued to practice using the Auric Shield for several months, it will remain in effect for twenty to thirty minutes before dropping back to the normal contours of your body.

Finally: To enhance the power of your Auric Shield, say, "God is; I am divinely protected now."

In reviewing the steps of the Law of Protection, the main points to remember are:

1. Empty your mind of all emotion and be in a state of peace.
2. Connect with your Higher Self by saying, "God is and I Am"
3. Use your Auric Shield as your protection for everything in your life. Always remember the power within you. You have been given this gift to use to your advantage. You make the choice to use it or not.

This procedure can only be used for good. It will not respond to anything negative.

The more you use it, the stronger it becomes.

CHAPTER 13

Four Steps into the Kingdom

Sometime in the 1960s, I turned to a television program where a rabbi, a priest, a Protestant minister and Baptist minister were discussing the location of the kingdom of God. I couldn't wait to hear their answers because I knew where it was, how simple it was, and the steps you took to get there.

The moderator asked each one if they could explain the location of the kingdom of God. The answers were diverse: *It's within. It's everywhere. It's above. It's in your mind.* They all sounded rather vague, which caused it to become a lengthy discussion.

The moderator asked, "Can you tell us where it is specifically?"

They couldn't answer. This didn't surprise me. I find that hardly anyone wants to talk about the kingdom of God or the kingdom of Heaven. Everyone stays away from this subject, as if it is impossible and unreasonable to understand. You can call it something else, but the word has the connotation of "having everything" in elegance, finery, affluence, and abundance in the physical. So, the kingdom of God means all of this and more. The "more" is all the things you can't see: love, peace, joy, fulfillment, etc., in the spiritual world.

I was there

Dr. Bussell explained the four steps into the kingdom.

The kingdom of God is not a geographical location, in itself, but a place—an actual place—a part of our mentality. It is there, but does it have a purpose? Is there a reason for its being there? Is it valuable to us if we know where it is, how to use it, and what to do about it? Yes, it most assuredly would!

The kingdom of God is within us, and is a place for us to go to and make a definite contact with God. It doesn't matter what you call the power that refers to God; the Presence, the Source, the Creator, Energy, or Life-giving Power, it always was and forever shall be. The Source is that which creates, governs, maintains, sustains, and contains all.

It doesn't cost anything, but it does give abundantly. There is not much preparation, and you learn to enter into the kingdom by doing it. So, there isn't very much left for us to wonder about except:

How do we get there?

How long does it take?

Why should we go?

When you go into the kingdom, you are getting in tune with the Infinite. You harmonize yourself with things that are real, not the things that are unreal.

Real means things that are eternal—truth, love, joy, etc. Unreal is anything that is temporary—disease, lack, unhappiness, etc. Jesus always saw that he was in the kingdom, in perfect harmony with God before he spoke the Word. And then he had the right results. We need to learn to always get into that same attitude when we expect to bring results.

Remember, when you go up the path into the kingdom, you go through four steps. You go through a change, and that change must be complete because you cannot go into the kingdom of God with things that are not of God's creation. When we get into the kingdom, into the Infinite, then we speak the Word. We state emphatically in our own consciousness that for which we are working. When you have made your statement, for instance, "I am radiant, vital, dynamic health" and hold that thought for a moment in the kingdom, there has to be a result. It cannot be otherwise.

However, if it is abundance you are working for, simply state, "I and my abundance are one, enough and to spare for every need." When you are in the kingdom, you are in harmony with abundance, tremendous abundance—much more than you ever need. While you are in harmony with supply, and if you continue in the attitude of abundance for some time when you come out of the kingdom, all of your needs will be supplied. Accept the fact that you can go into the kingdom, receive answers, direction, healing, or whatever you need, and come out with the wisdom to apply what you have received in your daily life. This is what Jesus meant when he said, "Go in and out and seek pasture." Seek wisdom, receive answers, and bring them into your daily life. If you have succeeded, this is where you are transformed. This is where your need is fulfilled: health, love, happiness, joy, peace, etc. This is the meaning of "It's your Father's good pleasure to give you the kingdom." *Father* was understood as protector, provider, kinder, wiser, most loving, and forgiving who was always present when you needed help.

Going into the kingdom of God is just as easy as getting warm when you come in from the cold. You can do it without even realizing it. An artist goes into the kingdom when he creates a painting, an actor when he is emoting a part, and a chef when he discovers a new recipe.

Now I will briefly explain a few points before I take you on the journey to the kingdom of God. The things that we know are the things over which we have power. If we don't know these things, we cannot do them because we have to know—and we have to know that we know—not just a little knowing, but knowing without a shadow of a doubt.

The secret is not to doubt because after you are ready, and you let doubt in, then you're going to be disappointed.

Another point, do not dictate how you are to receive. Your answer or blessing could come in many different ways, and do not put a limitation on your expectation.

If you are ready, I will now take you through the four steps into the kingdom of God.

The first step is to relax. Relax and let go. Let go of all negativity, emotion, judgments, and past unpleasant thoughts. Fully realize that we can't take anything negative into the kingdom of God. No disease, illness, or lack of harmony can stay in the kingdom. It doesn't belong there, and we can't keep it there, but this is what we can do. The structure of the brain is such that we can eliminate certain things and think of other things. We choose what we wish to think about. We use certain convolutions in the brain. Certain parts of our brain capacity are in use, and other parts are allowed to be dormant at the time.

You know how you try to remember something, and you go through a process searching in your brain to find the answer? This is the same process you go through to reach the kingdom. Let go, be calm, and have complete control of yourself. You can go through the relaxing exercise and be completely relaxed. Your blood pressure will change, your heart action will change, and your respiration will change. This is extremely important. In the brief thirty seconds it takes to go through the exercise, you can be completely relaxed, and you can do that anytime under any situation or circumstance, and be ready to go into the kingdom or get in tune with the Infinite.

In taking the second step, we go up the little path. How do we do that? Do we think we are going up a garden path? No, we are going through a pathway in the cranial process that leads to the upper part of the brain. When you start to think "up the little path," I want you to turn your eyes upward and concentrate on the mid part of your brain. (see diagram) When you focus on that particular part of your mind, your brain, you are sending your thought to that particular place. When you send it to any other part of your brain, you do not get the same result. When we start up the little path, we start by looking to that particular part of our brain and then through the little gate. At the pituitary gland, there is what is known as the "third eye," just back of the pituitary gland. There is a little tiny gap there. It is a very microscopic gap, and you pass through that particular gap. It won't be so difficult if we picture in our mind's eye the process of going up the little path, through the narrow gate, and pass between the third eye and the pituitary gland. Mentally, as we go through the narrow gate, we scrape off all barnacles of doubt, fear, anxiety, or any negative emotion.

The third step is through the Holy of Holies at the frontal brain, where there is a little expanse there and the convolutions all point in the same direction. It is the only expanse in the brain. Here we become as pure as we possibly can, as if clothed in white before we go into the kingdom of God. At the time when we pass through the Holy of Holies, there can be nothing but the spiritual thought left; we cannot get up there with anything else. When we pass through that, then we are ready to enter the kingdom of God.

The fourth and final step: the kingdom of God is the area at the top of the head, a little back of the center, which is the "soft spot" on the head of a baby. Then repeat the following words with love flowing from your heart: "And into the kingdom of God, where the power of God flows through us in righteousness. It is here that we are one with God, and we thank thee for hearing us for thou hearest us always, for leading us into the way of truth that frees, the perfect love that casteth out fear, the peace which passeth all understanding and the way of eternal life."

Dr. George E. Patterson, of the Patterson Therapy Center in Toluca Lake, California, gives us a biological explanation of the pathway created in your brain through this prayer.

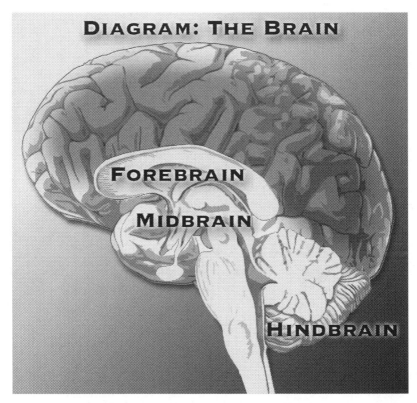

Forebrain, Midbrain, Hindbrain (Diagram).

The four steps constitute a diverse and holy prayer. Dr. Patterson frequently attended the Friday night meditation classes at Mrs. Ewing's home for more than ten years. The following is the biological explanation by Dr. Patterson:

> As the brain has been studied, research has pointed out that the function of the midbrain is basic to survival. It is referred to as our "reptilian brain" and explains that the "narrow path and the narrow gate" must go through the "midbrain" in order to reach the frontal lobe where higher cognition, reason, and consciousness are realized. Here is a complete description of how it actually works:
>
> In the Chirothesian prayer, Dr. Bussell describes our "going up the narrow path, through the narrow gate, into the kingdom of God where all is righteousness and we are one with the father."
>
> If you look at a picture of the brain, follow the path of the spinal column, up through the hindbrain (the brain stem, medulla, and pons area) to the midbrain, you will find that the midbrain is the "narrow gate" through which the energy and our thinking pass to reach the forebrain. The path has a physical correlation with our own bodies and refers to going up from that area in our center—the place from which our Harmony Center is located—into the spiritual center of our minds, which actually is in our forebrain.
>
> Picture in your mind taking the thought/energy/ harmony up the spinal cord and follow the path up the stem of the brain. (The brain stem is the autonomic part of our body, governing functions such as

breathing, heartbeat, and other basic functions that we don't have to think about.) This is the beginning of the path, i.e., "going up the narrow path."

Next is to go through the narrow gate as we visualize passing into and through the midbrain of the body. This part of the body is referred to as the reptilian brain and is made up of the "amygdala" and the "nucleus accumbens." There is no reasoning or logic here. It is a primitive brain and basic for our survival, i.e. "fight or flight!" When a stimulus comes, the midbrain says "run" or "fight" to survive! If our thinking is not relaxed and we are not centered, or if we are caught up in our thinking or ego, the midbrain "hijacks" our thinking and we cannot gain access to our true or higher selves in order to pass through the gate!

It is exactly this narrow gate through which we must pass in order to get to the kingdom of God and to be "one with the Father." Although the midbrain area helps us survive, if fed with anger or resentments, we cannot think clearly or have access to our true selves. We are not "right" with the Father and the true self within us. We do not have the ability to see that it is "our" thinking and that we are not "one with the Father." This is what behavioral scientists refer to as the "hijacked brain," which brings on a "fight-or-flight" reaction. We can't access the frontal lobe of our brain, where we are able to think and reason, to notice when we are out of sorts and not in harmony with God. Our oneness is "hijacked," and we cannot get there until we relax our minds and become "one with the Father."

Of course, "the plan is perfect," and we can see how it comes together in the Chirothesian Prayer: the relaxation, the breathing, the attitude of righteousness, and the harmony exercises are all designed to put us in a meditative state, help us lose our ego thought, and find God and oneness with the Creator.

Accordingly, both Dr. Bussell and Dr. Patterson explain that if we simply say the prayer and follow the path, we get there. The preparation is key in gaining the deeper and truer wisdom and oneness with God. This prayer and exercise will give you peace, truth, and grace. Follow and know it well. Practice and accept. Not only will your life be better, but you will be too.

And when your lifetimes are finished and all of your lessons are learned, you can say, "The show is over. Now I'm ready to go home."

CHAPTER 14

He Waited Eight Years

If after eight years of marriage you can't get pregnant even if you tried, and there aren't any remedies for infertility, what do you do?

I was thirty-six years old in 1958, and that was my dilemma. I noticed Robert was unhappy because we didn't have a child. At the Dover House Restaurant where he was working as manager, I would often notice Robert playing with the children, even carrying the ones he was familiar with. I could see his longing for a family. Although he didn't say anything to me, his feelings were obvious, and I realized something had to change.

Due to a physical condition, I was told that it would be difficult for me to conceive. According to society's standards, I was getting rather old to have children, and I decided to counsel with Dr. Bussell before time ran out.

As I sat in front of him relating my story about the years without conception, and the disappointment of not becoming pregnant, he listened intently and did not attempt to interrupt me. Before he spoke, Dr. Bussell looked deeply into my eyes, as if evaluating me, and said, quietly, "I've waited eight years for you to tell me this. You will be pregnant next month. You will have a little girl. She comes with much patience and a definite desire to have your husband as her father because they have an inward soul connection. She will be very good at math and excel in school."

"But Dr. Bussell,.....next month?...we haven't ...made love yet... I mean ..."

"Didn't you just tell me you wanted to have a child?" he said, as if to stop me from rambling on.

"Yes."

"That's all that's necessary."

However, I remained puzzled and not thoroughly convinced. Somehow, I thought this might be difficult for me to accomplish, so I asked him to mark on the calendar the right date for conception. He sighed, shook his head, smiled, and proceeded to mark the date. I'm sure he was exasperated, but knowing my nature, he managed to make allowances.

Two weeks later, on a Sunday after the service, I whispered in his ear, "Doctor, I just wanted you to know that ... we did it."

Dr. Bussell pulled back and looked rather shocked when he replied, "Nobody has ever told me that before."

I was embarrassed, but despite this feeling, I still managed to ask him to use his gift of vision to see if I was pregnant. He asked me to stand back, narrowed his eyes, observed, and nodded affirmatively. He had the ability to shift his vision, which allowed him to see the internal functioning of the body. That confirmation opened up the floodgates.

Everyone we knew was delighted to hear the news. Dr. Bussell also counseled that if we didn't have intercourse during the pregnancy, we would bring in a very evolved soul. An evolved soul is advanced mentally and spiritually. It didn't take us long to decide this is what we wanted. Consequently, we took his advice and were rewarded with an evolved soul. A baby is subject to all experiences and all emotions coming from the mother during pregnancy. Our responsibility was to stay in harmony, meditate every day, and be in an attitude of grateful anticipation of receiving a highly advanced soul. The more peace and love we felt, the greater health, happiness, and security the baby felt. If there was ever anything taking place that might be emotionally disturbing for me, I was not told. This kept me in a happy, healthy, peaceful state, which was more in keeping with the energy of this new, desired soul.

In the third month of pregnancy, I was awakened in the night by what looked like a bright white light edged in blue. It moved from the doorway and hovered over my head. At first, it grew larger and then began to diminish and disappear. I had no fear, but I was curious about the meaning of the phenomenon. I was sure there was some kind of a message, and I didn't want to miss it. I wondered if Robert had seen it, but I didn't want to awaken him. The following morning, he was first to ask me if I had seen the white light in the night. I was relieved. I thought I might have been hallucinating.

On Friday afternoon, we attended the two o'clock meditation. After the service, we approached Dr. Bussell for a possible explanation of what we had seen.

With a smile, he said, "Oh, that was your daughter checking you out."

I understood exactly what he meant; it was her soul. What a wonderful blessing to be able to view her soul even before she was born.

Dr. Bussell explained that the baby isn't an independent living being until the soul attaches itself to the body. And how does it do that? First of all, the baby is considered stillborn until it takes a breath.

On September 11, 1960, during Dr. Bussell's lesson on divine law, we read Genesis 2:7. "And the Lord God formed man out of the dust of the ground, and breathed into his nostrils the breath of life; and man became a living soul."

Dr. Bussell said, "When you were born, you did not breathe, but suddenly something happened: you gasped for breath. The soul then attached itself to your body, and you became a living soul, exactly like the first man and woman, and everyone since that time. The soul attaches itself to the body near the spleen when the baby takes the first breath. And the soul leaves the body when expelling the last breath."

Life is so much easier when you know the truth, I thought.

During my pregnancy, we moved to a two-story house in the hills, overlooking Hollywood. I had morning sickness and had to spend some of the time in bed. We were having a section of the house painted, and even though the paint fumes were much stronger in the other part of the house, I was in the bedroom where the fumes were still too strong for comfort. I had a headache that wouldn't stop and felt nauseous. Exhausted and ill, I tried desperately to open the old French windows to let in fresh air, but they were covered by layers of paint from years of disuse, and they were impossible to open.

There was no possibility of opening them. The paint fumes in the other part of the house were worse, and with nothing else left to do, I stayed in bed and prayed for help. I wondered if my thoughts were strong enough that Dr. Bussell would hear me and help me open the window.

As I was lying there with my hands over my face, I heard a sharp cracking sound. I opened my eyes and gasped when I saw the French window slowly open. I thought I was dreaming. I got up to inspect the window. On the floor, I found large chunks of paint that had prevented it from opening. I could hardly believe my eyes. What a relief! I was full of gratitude. I thanked Dr. Bussell when I saw him.

He said, "Please don't thank me. Thank God. I had nothing to do with it."

Pregnancy isn't fun. Having a common cold while pregnant is very uncomfortable. Naturally, I did everything in my power to avoid catching one. I must say I did very well until the woman next to me in my exercise class came in with a cold. There is a saying, "What you fear comes upon you," meaning what you fear, you will experience. I had fear I would catch her cold, therefore, I came down with a miserable cold. I didn't realize at the time, but I was very angry with the woman in the class for not only having a cold and coming to class, but for sitting next to me.

After a few days of discomfort and not being able to breathe or sleep, I called Dr. Bussell for help. My call was not returned, and I was frantic. I even tried a trip to Palm Springs in the 104-degree heat, hoping it would bring some relief. It didn't.

I finally gave up the struggle, and I went to Friday's meditation even though I could hardly breathe. During the lesson, my breathing relaxed, and the congestion left my body. Oh! What a relief! I could breathe again.

When I reached Dr. Bussell after the meditation service to thank him since I knew he had sent healing energy, he replied, "I'm sorry I couldn't help you before. You were too angry."

My anger was, apparently, blocking all the healing energy Dr. Bussell was sending. This was a good lesson about what anger can do—and the enormous power it can have over us. It wasn't until I attended the meditation service and relaxed that I was able to let go of the anger and receive help.

A friend and fellow minister, Dr. Fletcher Harding, taught me that anger preserves the ego. After you think about it, and how it relates to incidents and people, you know it's true. Anger creates acid in the body, clouds the mind, eliminates friendship, loses jobs, and causes us to have heart attacks, body imbalances, etc.

I was there

When our "littlest angel" was born, there was much elation among our friends and relatives. But all was not roses since our new baby angel had colic, and we were up until four o'clock one morning, walking the floor, trying to get her to sleep. Finally, we gave up and called Dr. Bussell at home (which no one does unless there is an emergency). Our baby was asleep by the time we ended the call. When we took her in for Dr. Bussell's observation and evaluation, he found a small sigmoid that was preventing the milk from passing through easily. He healed her.

Another time, she wouldn't stop crying no matter what I did, and I couldn't figure out what was wrong. Again, I called to seek advice from Dr. Bussell, and he told me there was something caught in her throat. He told me to melt a little butter and put it on her tongue to clear her throat. I did, and the problem was solved.

The lesson of "waiting" and being patient has carried me through my life. Even though my beloved teacher is no longer on this earth plane, his words always come to me many times when things seem to be going wrong and the stress level builds.

There is a lesson and answer in every experience if we stop and observe. I learned to step aside from my ego and impatience and let the right action take place. This is where we learn to "let go and let God." If we ask and become silent, the answer or help comes when we need it, and in just the right way.

When we close one door, God opens another for us to step through and explore.

Dr. Bussell in full robe, receiving confirmation of his Mastership.

SCREEN AND STAGE

Los Angeles Times   SUNDAY, JULY 29, 1945

BEVERLY WARREN—Plays in "Motel Wives," light comedy fare recently opened at the Musart Theater.

The early years. Making it into the trade papers.

The three Stooges and me "The Three Loan Wolves."
Courtesy Columbia Picture Corporation. Copyright 1946.

"DOA," starring Edmond O'Brian. I'm the serious one on the left. Courtesy United Artists Corporation. Copyright 1949.

"River Lady," starring Yvonne DeCarlo and Dan Duryea. I'm the one wearing the black dress on the left. Courtesy Columbia Picture Corporation. Copyright 1949.

The Chirothesia Church during choir practice. The symbol of the cross represents man upright with arms outstretched, and the "C" is in the form of a snake representing the wisdom in Chirothesia.

With my daughter Greta.

Teaching a group of students at one of my seminars.

CHAPTER 15

Time to Leave

If there is a perfect time for everything, why are we always in such a hurry to do everything?

Have you noticed how we wish or expect things to happen instantly? We even want flowers to bloom sooner. However, if we force a rosebud to open, the flower will surely die. We came into this expression of life at the right time, and we will leave at the right time. There's a perfect time to enter and a perfect time to depart. This was exemplified in the life of Dr. Bussell.

He was such an adoring husband to Mrs. Bussell. Even though he was counseling and healing weekdays from six in the morning until nine at night, held an afternoon meditation on Friday, and conducted a service on Sunday, he always managed to spend time with his wife.

Mrs. Bussell had a palsy condition, and it wasn't easy for her to walk. When she suffered her tenth stroke, the doctors said she would not last the night. Dr. Bussell simply walked out of his wife's hospital room. Mrs. Bussell's relatives were shocked at his reaction, but they didn't know that Dr. Bussell was searching for an empty room in which to pray. There was too much emotion emanating from his wife's relatives, and the atmosphere was not peaceful. He knew he had to separate himself in order to be at one with the power of Universal Love, a level of consciousness in peace where no negation exists and where change can take place.

He prayed that if the Law of God would let his wife live, he would teach her the lessons she still needed to learn. His prayer was granted, and even though she remained bedridden, he sat by her side every night to silently teach her. Mrs. Bussell lived another year before peacefully making her transition.

With all that Dr. Bussell knew—the healings and the miracles—you would think it would be easier for him to be separated from Mrs. Bussell. After all, he had the ability to contact both sides of life. However, such was not the case. I called him one afternoon to ask how he was, and I was surprised to hear so much sadness in his voice. I tried to comfort him. "But Dr. Bussell, you said there is no separation."

"There isn't. But I'm still in the body, and while in the physical body, you still have emotions. I can feel that she wants me with her, but she won't let me contact her."

A year later, I was not ready to accept the truth that Dr. Bussell was preparing for his own transition. Before he left the church to put his affairs in order, he called me in for a consultation.

"Mrs. Gaard, will you promise me something?" he asked.

I was anxious to comply since he had never asked anything of me before. "Of course," I answered. "Anything."

"There is something you are going to want to do, but promise me you won't do it."

I was puzzled and confused.

He said, "If you do this, your husband will take you back, but he'll never forget. If you do as I say, you will be glad you did."

He didn't elaborate, and I was so shocked I couldn't think to ask questions. From the little he did say, I understood that I would meet someone and want to leave my marriage, but in the long run, it wouldn't work out, and I would want to return to my husband. His statements were very alarming because I knew that Dr. Bussell was always right.

Right then and there, I knew I had to keep my promise.

Soon after our conversation, Dr. Bussell left the church to prepare for his transition. We were all stunned and numbed by the experience. All of us knew better than to express any emotion since we wanted him to be free with no strings attached.

Dr. Bussell's mission was completed. He had taught so many people in his church and many others all over the world how to live and transform their lives by his example. Whenever anyone associated with the church left or moved away from the area, the vacancy was always filled.

He said, "God never leaves a void. It will always be filled, if we let it. The Essenes taught that 'letting' was an initiation into the spirit of God; however, this seemed to be the most difficult to achieve."

When I realized that "letting" meant "allowing," it changed my attitude, and I was better able to accept the things that crossed my path. Dr. Bussell made his transition on March 7, 1962, the day after Robert's birthday. I know he arranged it that way so that Robert never had a sad remembrance on his birthday.

The impact of Dr. Bussell's passing did not take effect for some time. I think he must have wrapped all of us in so much peace that we were unaware of the separation. However, when the full realization took effect, there was an emptiness and loss without his presence on earth that nothing would fill. Confusion resulted at the church when we awakened to his loss. People were scrambling for anything that belonged to Dr. Bussell—any souvenir that belonged to him left on the church property.

It seems as though we need to see and know someone physical who can show us the way. By witnessing a living example, we will have more faith that maybe we too can demonstrate the same.

Ann Woodall, Dr. Bussell's secretary, was with him during his last six months, putting everything in order. Ann related a very personal story to me when she came to babysit Greta one evening.

On the second day after his transition, Ann said she heard a knock on her apartment door. When she opened the door, there stood Dr. Bussell. She was overcome with surprise and joy. She begged him to come in and sit down. He entered and made himself comfortable.

"Oh, Doctor," she said full of excitement. "I'm so happy to see you. What can I do for you?"

He explained what he wanted her to do with his personal items, and she immediately complied with his wishes. Ann knew Dr. Bussell enjoyed a cup of coffee, so she asked if she could serve him.

"Yes, thank you," he answered. "That would be nice."

With great love and care, she prepared his coffee, talking to him all the while. But when she returned from the kitchen, he had disappeared. Ann was filled with mixed emotions. With Dr. Bussell gone, there was nothing else for her to do but make sure to carry out his instructions to the best of her ability.

Everyone attended the funeral service, and the casket was left open for us to view our teacher and spiritual advisor one more time. As I passed the casket, I felt a wave of heat emanating from his body; it was as if he was still expressing his love for us.

One of my friends, Lillian, was also a member of the church. While she was away temporarily in New York, she met a man who she wanted to marry. When she related the miracles that Dr. Bussell had performed, her fiancé refused to accept the legitimacy of her stories. Lillian had wanted him to meet this remarkable man and see his warm and loving smile. She was devastated at the thought that her fiancé would never know this wonderful man who changed everyone's lives.

Dr. Bussell knew they were returning, and he also knew of her fiancé's disbelief. As absurd as it sounds, when her fiancé was passing the casket, Dr. Bussell broke into a beautiful smile. Her fiancé thought he was seeing things, and he went around to view the body again. The same thing happened. When he told Lillian, she went back also, but no one else saw Dr. Bussell's smile.

When we all converged in the parking lot, Lillian's fiancé was visibly shaken. He kept repeating, "Believe me. It's true. Believe me. It's true."

We never disbelieved him. We all knew it was true. It was he who had to believe.

Many unusual things happened, as though in a blink of an eye, during this period. I could not understand many of them. There were sudden healings, misunderstandings were corrected, and people's minds were suddenly changed. I knew there was a higher energy at work.

It was difficult to find someone to fill Dr. Bussell's shoes, and the church was in turmoil for several years. We were constantly vigilant, tirelessly searching for a suitable replacement, but none could fill the void.

Ann recalled something Dr. Bussell had said to her just before he made the transition, and it saddened her deeply. With tears in his eyes, he had said, "My little church is going to die." Unfortunately, this turned out to be quite prophetic.

For a long time after the last few remaining followers either expired or moved away, the church stood in ruins. Only the heading above the pulpit remained, with the words, "Ye Shall Know the Truth; and the Truth Shall Make you Free, John 8:32."

Over the years several offers were made to purchase the church building, and the property was sold in 1994. It was soon demolished to make way for an apartment complex.

Dr. Bussell had placed a note in a sealed vial underneath the cornerstone of the church when it was built. He said this note contained a single word that was the answer for every condition in man's life, and he wanted the vial to be retrieved when the church was demolished. We all waited anxiously as one of the ministers dug it up and carefully opened the vial. We tried to guess, but no one was right. The word was *faith*.

Immediately, I thought, *If you have faith as a grain of mustard seed, nothing shall be impossible to you.*

We were all well aware of the meaning, and it was as if Dr. Bussell was speaking to each one of us personally. I had enough faith to know life is continuous. I also had enough faith to know we could apply the Universal Law and transform any situation. Sometimes the one we depend on must leave so we can begin to practice what we know, and thus, finally stand with both feet firmly planted on the ground.

CHAPTER 16

Absent Treatments

Have you ever had something happen that was so unusual that you couldn't possibly explain it, even if you tried? You knew it really happened, but how are you going to explain it to someone else when they say it was just a coincidence, and it didn't really happen?

I know what it feels like because I was there. At the time it happened, I took it for granted, and it didn't seem that unusual. But now, after all these years, I realize that a miraculous blessing took place right in front of my eyes.

When Robert was diagnosed with pancreatic cancer, I wanted to know how and why Robert had developed this. I knew there was a reason for every disease. I researched and inquired of many people, including doctors, highly trained nurses, and professionals in metaphysical science.

I dug up Robert's history and found that his insecurity from being placed in a foster home as a child created a deep-seated fear. During his active duty in World War II, he became deeply depressed and never sought help. Instead, he turned to alcohol. He was previously married to a selfish woman who only wanted his money and then left him. Robert was never one to communicate or release any of his feelings. He left them buried deep within. Through my research, I found the deepest place hidden in the body is the pancreas.

If we bury negative emotions within our consciousness, without understanding and releasing, it will result in the form of a disease until the lesson is learned. The best way to avoid this type of problem is to talk about your feelings or write about them in a journal. This helps to empty out destructive negative emotions. Another approach is an absent treatment.

A treatment is a procedure to relieve a condition. If you apply an ice pack to an aching muscle, it is a treatment. If you give encouragement, positive support, and prayer to a person, it is also called a treatment. One is referred to as a physical treatment, and the latter is an absent treatment. The following is what Dr. Bussell shared on this subject:

> In treating at a distance, or what metaphysicians call absent treatment, thought is more rapid and potent than words. Thought does not know time and space, while a word or audible sound belongs on the material plane and must traverse space and endure in time in order to reach its destination. Notice how instantly your thought is at the sun, the center of the Earth, or at any other place. Thought does not travel; it is already there. Every fact in spirit is already there, and further, it is already in evidence. To see this is to lift yourself into this fact. To see it for another is to lift him or her into it. If I am lifted up to the plane of reality, it draws all things into this realm.

Dr. Bussell gave both physical and absent treatments. We all have the same opportunity once we learn how to focus, concentrate, and ignore interfering thoughts. If you have thoughts and emotions about your illness, and I only have a perfect thought and picture of your perfect health, I am giving you an absent treatment. My thought agrees with the Law of God, which is perfect, radiant, vital, and dynamic health. If you accept this truth, you will quickly improve.

Robert's diagnosis came fourteen years after Dr. Bussell had made his transition, but Dr. Bussell foresaw Robert's health condition even before it had manifested and left a series of absent treatments for Robert to draw upon whenever a need arose. It was only after Robert's diagnosis that Dr. Bussell's assistant made us aware of these absent treatments.

The absent treatments Dr. Bussell left for Robert consisted of a gentle vibration moving through the body, relaxing, and eliminating any apparent pain. There were nights when this vibration was felt as we were sleeping.

One night, a gentle movement of the bed awakened me. Robert was also very much aware of when it happened. All he had to do was mentally ask for a treatment, and the vibration would begin. It was a miraculous blessing for both of us.

When the series of treatments was completed, Robert was taken to the veterans' hospital, and he remained there for two months before making his transition.

My dearest friend Sheila, an angel of love and one of the original seven students, went to the hospital. She continued the healing vibration by the laying on of hands, during the last weeks of Robert's life. Robert's last words were, "I've never had any pain." It was a blessing and relief for me to hear this.

Greta and I sat in his hospital room and had our last good-byes as Robert took his last breath. Greta said she saw his soul exit from the crown at the top of his head—a trailing white mist that disconnected from his body and disappeared through the ceiling.

At the time, I wondered why Robert wasn't healed, but later, I realized that you never interfere with the perfect divine plan. When someone has a terminal illness, like Robert had, there are lessons to be learned and changes to be made for personal growth. This is a time to go into consciousness, review your life, evaluate your mistakes, and recognize the lesson. It's a time to learn and let healing take place before you make the transition.

Dr. Bussell's absent treatments relieved Robert of his pain, and they gave Robert the wisdom needed to understand his lesson.

On his hospital tray, Robert left a note.

> *I was lying here, watching the nurses walk down the hall, and I saw myself on a stage, playing a part of a man dying of cancer. I asked God, "If this is all a stage, and we are all actors, why life?" And He said, "As long as there are questions, there will be life."*

I cried when I read this since I knew it was the voice of God.

CHAPTER 17

Is the Hummingbird Present?

When does the soul graduate? And what does this mean? The soul doesn't die. The word *graduate* means to move to another level in life's expression.

Two years after Dr. Bussell graduated, Greta was four, and I was so busy as a housewife and mother that I didn't take a moment to feel empty. I investigated and found everyone else felt empty, too. It seems as though we were all kept so busy that we didn't feel the loss. However, I was feeling the impact of the blessings and miracles in my life. I had meditated and constantly searched for a teacher for so long. Now I needed to find something to replace what I had lost, but I didn't know where to go. It seemed my attempt was futile; no one could take Dr. Bussell's place. What was I to do? I had lost my direction.

In my desperation, I began tearing wallpaper off the walls in the entry hall of my home. In my mind, I was screaming, "What do you want me to do?" I kept repeating it until my hands were sore and I was exhausted.

After the third day of this irrational, emotional behavior, I heard a loud voice in my mind—a voice that wasn't my own. "You're going to teach what you have learned."

I quickly answered, "No, not me. I'm not ready!" I fought with this voice for several days until I realized from the silence that this was not a suggestion. It was an assignment I could not deny.

The seven people who came forth were interested in how I maintained my attitude, peace, and sense of humor under pressure. When I shared the understanding of the Universal Laws and how to live daily and take control of life, they all asked me to teach what I knew.

I began teaching the seven students at Robert's office, one night a week. I would read a lesson, and we would have discussions.

After three days, my inner voice said, "Now close the book, and tell them the lesson."

I was so afraid that I wanted to quit, right then and there. I didn't feel I knew enough to teach off the top of my head. I felt more confident reading Dr. Bussell's lessons word for word, but I knew the only way to truly teach the Universal Laws was to teach from what I had learned—from my own experiences—and not from a lesson book. Unfortunately, I didn't feel ready and doubted my ability to continue. I went on a weekend retreat by the ocean to be quiet and meditate.

Again, I asked of Divine Intelligence, "Please give me a sign that I may know, without a shadow of a doubt, you want me to carry on this teaching of the Law of God and how to live it in our daily lives."

After three days of total silence, I was ready to give up. But then, I decided to change my attitude, to "let go and accept." I went to the courtyard, where it was still and quiet. I was alone. There were no trees or flowers nearby, and I was standing peacefully in the sunlight. It was early in the afternoon, and there was a gentle ocean breeze. I closed my eyes and just became grateful for everything.

I was there

Without opening my eyes, I heard a fluttering noise very close to my face. A joy swept over me. I knew this was my answer. Carefully, I opened my eyes without moving; to my surprise, I saw a hummingbird at the end of my nose. His tiny black eyes were looking straight into mine. I wanted to gasp, but I knew if I did, he would disappear. He hovered there as long as I could hold my breath. When I blinked, he was gone. I quickly looked left and right to see where he went, but there were no trees or anyplace for him to go. I was sad to have him leave, but I was happy because I knew it was my answer. I was fulfilling my destiny and was on the right path.

The following week, I gave a class and told them the story about my experience with the hummingbird. While in the middle of the story, someone gasped and pointed to the glass sliding door. A hummingbird was fluttering his little wings and trying to get in. This was not the only time a hummingbird appeared to me or to my students. Whenever, there was a special need or someone in the class needed support, a hummingbird appeared as a sign.

One of my students who was extremely anxious about a recent medical issue was waiting in the doctor's exam room for results from a test when he looked out and saw a hummingbird on the other side of the window. Not only were there no flowers or trees around, the exam room was on the tenth floor! Hummingbirds are not known to fly very high above the ground; they tend to fly just above the treetops. This hummingbird flew ten stories high, and it served as a sign to my student that everything was going to be okay.

The hummingbird—the expression of beauty, love, and grace—is always present when you need an answer. Just watch for it!

CHAPTER 18

The End Is the Beginning

As I write this final chapter, forty-eight years have passed since my teacher left this plane of existence. My daughter is fifty-three, a college professor and worldwide speaker on ecology and women's rights. She's written four books and is a mother to my gregarious granddaughter.

Before Robert passed, he turned to me and said, "You will be married again."

He was right. Twelve years after Robert's transition, I married an actor and teacher, much like myself. I am sure Robert would approve of my new husband. Charles and I have now been married for as long as I was married to Robert!

After Dr. Bussell's transition, my purpose and assignment was to teach what I had learned, which I have done for forty years. Although I am now semiretired, I continue to conduct an advanced class of enlightened students, who are a few of the thousands that have studied.

The National Academy of Metaphysics and the Universal Laws, are teachings that are practiced all over the world.

You probably wonder if I hear from my teacher. The answer is yes. Whenever there is a dire need, a hummingbird, a thought, a sound, a voice, or a person appears to give me a message, an answer I was too preoccupied to hear.

As we conclude our journey together in this final chapter, and as you apply all the lessons you have learned in this book, you will be rewarded with a new beginning of a new life. This is the ending of the old one and a beginning of a different way of life that will set you free of negative patterns that have limited and prevented your freedom and enlightenment. The fifteen minutes you take in the morning in order to increase and strengthen your health, set your day in harmony and protection, and open the door to a greater abundance will adjust your timing so that you will be in the right place at the right time with the right people. It is well worth the effort of creating a routine that will change your life for greater happiness and freedom. It is my belief that this is not the only life we live. Millions of others have the same belief. This being the truth, we conclude that whenever we make a positive move, we are setting the foundation for a future, better life.

If we stop and look around, we shall see that our lives are full of established procedures. We have daily and weekly routines. We have yearly routines of making New Year's resolutions. We set times and deadlines for what we want to accomplish. If we miss appointments, our entire schedules suffer. It will always have an effect on our lives, whether we realize it or not. If we aren't on time, we will have a lesson to learn because someone we depended on may not be on time for us.

If you create a habit of setting your meditation at the same time every morning, what you need will always be "on time." This could be called good karma. What you do, will be done unto you."

My pet squirrel is at the sliding door every morning at 7:30 to receive his peanuts. I don't know how he knows the time, but if I'm not there, he leaves and doesn't return that day. If we aren't where we are supposed to be at a specified time, we could miss the opportunity of a lifetime.

You can reinvent your life if something goes wrong or not according to plan. If things haven't worked in your life, you have the opportunity to practice what you have learned to transform your life from a dead end to a new beginning.

I will suggest nine steps to remember when carrying out your meditation:

1. cleansing breath
2. four steps into the kingdom of God
3. ten-count breathing
4. health and healing
5. harmony
6. gratitude
7. abundance
8. Auric Shield
9. closing prayer

The Essenes, the most spiritually evolved people on earth, began every day with meditation by setting the right thoughts and attitudes to create their days, and you can do the same. If you have disturbing thoughts or dreams, you can empty out all of the confusion or negativity by using the proper breathing procedure and expelling the breath forcefully.

If you have disagreements, you can retreat and harmonize yourself and your situation. It's exciting to see how things change when you spread the Harmony: arguments cease, people become more pleasant, confrontations mellow, and even dogs cease to bark. This is your miraculous gift.

Keep in mind that it's always time to be grateful. Every day, you can find some small blessing to be thankful for. It's easy to be grateful for large blessings, but gratitude blossoms in small ones.

Dr. Bussell said, "Even be grateful for a beautiful gray day!"

Before a manifestation, expressing gratitude is accepting the Law of Abundance. The law never changes, but our comprehension and application of the law changes.

Thoughts are significant and capable of creating powerful effects. What is your first thought in the morning? If you want your life to change, realize that your first thought will direct your day. If you set your goal for the day and put it in Right Action, the Universal Law will set in motion your desire and bring about the perfect manifestation at the right time for the good of all. Always keep your final goal in mind, and every step you take will bring you closer to your heart's desire.

Before retiring for the night, place a book or an item in your visual field beside your bed. In the morning, before you step out of bed, you will remember to make your connection with the power that created you. "I and God are One. God is; I am." This immediately connects you to the Creative Cosmic Principle, and you realize who you are and why you are here.

You are here to fulfill your destiny, that which you came to accomplish. Expand your experience and grow in wisdom to discover and share the talents you have been given in this lifetime. You are here to relieve human suffering and learn what the energy called love really is. Learn how to love unconditionally, and most of all, live in harmony by observing and applying the Universal Laws of God in your daily life. We do not live for ourselves alone. We live to share, serve, and grow with others.

Life is simple if you know the law. You don't need a college degree to tap into the source and get the right answers. You have six very important laws to help you along the way. Life gives you the experience to prove what you have learned. Nothing happens overnight. Everything takes time, which is the unfolding of God's perfect plan for you. Don't look at your life as an ending. It is a beginning—a beginning of a new way of life that enables you to enjoy the endless adventure in your journey through eternity.

This is my gift to you!

CHAPTER 19

Directed Meditation

This meditation was practiced daily by the Essenes. During the forty years in which he studied the Essene teachings, Dr. Bussell compiled the various laws into this directed meditation, and today, thousands of people use this method in their daily lives. In only fifteen minutes, you will feel that all of your needs have been met.

Prepare your day with the first thought as you awaken. If you need to remember, place a book on the floor where you will stand. Let your first thought be, "God Is; I am." With this, you have made your connection with the power within you. Repeat it throughout the day as you need to. Freshen yourself, and then open the door or window to do the cleansing breath. As you inhale and exhale seven fast puffs of breath, you have expelled any negative energy or emotions you have accumulated during the night.

First Step: Location

Choose the same quiet location for meditation every day. It is best to do this meditation first thing in the morning, with no food or drink in your stomach. Put your feet flat on the floor and your hands palm down in your lap with your spine erect and your head tall. Breathe slowly and deeply, but do not be concerned with your breath. Let go! Let go! Let go of every thought in your mind, every emotion, every feeling. Just let them dissolve into nothing, and go deep within yourself, the one self, the one mind. Keeping your attention between your eyebrows lovingly, and holding your gaze steady with your eyes closed will still your mind.

Second Step: Relaxation

Begin to relax now. Relax the top of your head, your face, and the back of your head, neck, and shoulders. Relax any tension in your arms, hands, upper back, and chest. Let go! Let go of any tightness or tension in your lower back, abdomen, hips, thighs, knees, calves, legs, ankles, and feet. Take a nice slow deep breath now and just let go!—and let God! Recognize that there is only one mind, one Power, one Presence, and we come together in this one thought, and one recognition of the truth that sets us free, remembering that "with God, all things are possible now."

Third Step: Prayer

Visualize being led up the little path (explained in Dr. Patterson's diagram), through the narrow gate (corresponding to your hairline), through the Holy of Holies (frontal area, the only vacuum in the brain, where you become totally clear and ready to be one with God), and into the kingdom of God (up to the location of the soft spot on a newborn baby's head), where all is righteousness (right—use—ness). Here, we are One with God. "We thank thee for hearing us. Thou hearest us always, and we thank thee for leading us into the way of the truth that frees.

The perfect love that casts out all fear. The peace that passeth all understanding and the way of eternal life. Amen."

Fourth Step: Breath

(Stand) For our ten-count breathing, recognize that as we breathe, we bring in the vital crystals out of the air—the natural vitamins—as we inhale very slowly to the count of ten. In your mind, count to ten. Swallow the breath (this sends oxygen to the cranial process of the brain), exhale, and count slowly to ten. Take a normal breath, inhale, and exhale, and repeat two more times so that you have completed this exercise for a total of three times. Now you are reenergized and ready to meditate.

Fifth Step: Health

Be seated and resume your position with your attention centered lovingly between your eyebrows. Visualize the rising sun, this beautiful red orange color, for this is the color of vibrant health. Let this color heal every part of your body. See it and feel it as you say, "God is; I am, radiant, vital, dynamic health now."

Let this shower of red-orange diamonds filter through every gland and muscle of your body, reenergizing and rejuvenating every part of you. And as you reaffirm, "God is; I am, radiant, vital, dynamic health now," you become the perfect image of health. Hold a moment. If anyone has asked for your help in prayer, you may now see them perfect, the way they were created. We never do this unless asked to do so. There may be lessons to be learned, and we are not to interfere with anyone's soul path. We express gratitude and ask that they are receptive to the help directed toward them.

Sixth Step: Harmony

Now, let us go to our Harmony Center. Imagine a line was drawn from your left lower shoulder point to your right lower shoulder point—at the place where the line crosses your spine—that is the location of your Harmony Center. It's a vibration, a tone you were given at the time you were born. It never changes. It's your gift; it's your inheritance. Harmony! You can create harmony anytime you reestablish this exercise. Let us do that now.

When you think to that place, you will automatically go to that place. If you were clairvoyant, you would see a light, an off-white light, edged in blue. It moves like the liquid in a thermometer. As you pick up the tone, through your thoughts, you can move that vibration—the light—that continues up your spine, vertebra by vertebra, up the back of the neck, and to the top of your head. Let that tone vibration fill your mind, your brain, putting every thought in harmony. See that light, like a laser beam going through your mind, purifying, clearing, and harmonizing every thought.

Take the tone—the light—down the left side of your neck, down the left arm, elbow, wrist, fingers, and thumb. Leave the tone in the center of your left hand. You might feel a tingling sensation there. Return to your Harmony Center in thought, pick up the tone again, move it up the spine, vertebra by vertebra, up the back of your neck to the top of the head. Carry it again, down the left side of your head and neck, but this time, come down through the left shoulder, past the left side of the spine, reaching every nerve. Come down over the left hip, thigh, knee, calf, ankle, and foot. Leave your tone in the center of your left foot. Again, you may feel a tingling sensation. Now you have filled the left side of your body.

Think to the Harmony Center and pick it up again. Move that light tone up the spine, to the top of the head. This time, move down the right side of the neck, right shoulder, and come down the right arm, elbow, forearm, wrist, fingers, and thumb. Leave your tone in the center of your right hand. Return to your Harmony Center and pick up the tone, moving it up the spine to the top of the head. This time, come down the right side of your neck and down the right shoulder, past the right side of the spine, over the right hip, thigh, knee, calf, ankle, and foot. Leave your tone in the center of your right foot.

Return again to your Harmony Center and pick up the tone for the last time, taking it up the spine to the top of your head. This time, as you come down the back of your head, vertebra by vertebra, you will activate the root of each chakra (or energy center) as you come down the spine. Each chakra will begin to spin, creating the harmony, which is yours. Follow the tone right down to the tip of your spine and bring that light tone into the pelvic area, through the stomach, solar plexus, and all the organs in that area. Come up into your heart, letting there be harmony in your heart, chest, and lungs. Come up through the throat, the facial cavities, and back to the top of your head.

Now we have traversed all the great nerve trunks of the body. We visited every ganglia. Say, "I am perfect harmony." Every nerve and nervelet carries perfect harmony to every cell of your body. And now having established your own perfect harmony, if there are those that we would help in harmony, name them, and realize universal harmony for each of them.

This is the only exercise that relaxes every nerve. Now that you have become perfect harmony, you have re-created that which already is. You can also recognize it right where you are, the place where you live. See perfect harmony throughout every room, through everyone there—perfect universal harmony—for you are a unit of God's universal harmony.

Take a moment to go to the place where you work to see harmony among all of your fellow workers, friends, relatives, and loved ones. Recognize this perfect universal harmony taking place now in our world—in every man, woman, and child. Recognize all of nature; see it, feel it, know it. Let it reach all the places that need it the most, the people who need it the most, and filter—as diamonds of light—right through the very center of Mother Earth, and far into space, which is the realm of God.

As you look back, you can see that there is a light around the Earth, edged in blue. This is how the Earth looks when it is in harmony. Very gently now, return to this place, and be grateful from your heart for some small blessing this day. Be truly grateful. Be grateful for all things given and all things taken; these are all blessings. We recognize that gratitude opens the door to abundance.

Seventh Step: Abundance

We cannot receive our abundance unless we are grateful. Accept your own abundance, which is "enough and to spare" for your every need now. Apple green is the color of abundance. The world is full of color. The Earth is covered with this color. Keep this color in mind, and surround yourself with this vibration of abundance. Make it personal.

"I and my abundance are one, enough and to spare and to share for my every need now." Share this thought with someone who needs this help, and see their every need fulfilled by God.

Eighth Step: Right Action

Let's take these thoughts and place them in Right Action. Right Action is God's love in motion.

> I release and let go into God's perfect divine right action, my life, the plan of my life, and my thoughts. I know I am in the right place at the right time with the right people for my highest good and the good of all. I know perfect Right Action is taking place right now, and I accept this, for I know I am an inseparable part of the power that created me perfect. It's the Father's good pleasure to give us the kingdom. Thank you for hearing me, thou hearest me always. Amen.

ABOUT THE AUTHOR

Beverly Jane Weichel was born in Omaha, Nebraska, in 1923. Even as a child, she searched for a teacher to enlighten her and show her the path back to her consciousness. Along the way, she became a Presbyterian and an Episcopalian, received sacraments in Catholicism, and converted to Judaism before becoming a Chirothesian, which encompasses all religions.

Beverly moved from the Midwest to California to pursue acting and modeling. Once in Hollywood, Beverly was a couture model for upscale fashion designers. She performed at the Hollywood Canteen and garnered several roles on stage and in the movies. She even landed the coveted role of Molly, the gangster's moll, in the Three Stooges' *Three Loan Wolves*.

Beverly also traveled with actor Edward G. Robinson's wife in the Desert Battalion, a group of starlets who entertained the soldiers in camps around California, and she was a chaplain in actress Jane Russell's charity Women's Adoption International Fund (WAIF) to adopt children abroad. While under contract to a commercial film company in Colorado, Beverly met her first husband, Robert.

Beverly's search for a teacher was over when she met Dr. DJ Bussell. He was a renowned world teacher, healer, traveler, attorney, and translator of Aramaic, Hebrew, and Sanskrit, and he spent more than sixty years studying and translating the ancient records of the Essenes.

Beverly studied under the tutelage of Dr. Bussell for eight years, and after his transition, she continued his vision and became president of A Way of Life with centers in Sherman Oaks, Palm Springs, and Big Bear, California, as well as Lake Whitney, Texas, and Kona, Hawaii.

Beverly was also a media personality with a popular radio show (*The Time Is Now*) and a television show (*Inherit Your Wealth*) in Los Angeles and Palm Springs, California.

Beverly received a doctor of philosophy degree and has taught and lived the Universal Laws set down by the Essenes for sixty years. She has transformed many lives and is acknowledged for her work in several books.

To reach Dr. Beverly J. Gaard directly, please write to her at:
A Way of Life
P.O. Box 1254
Studio City, CA 91614
iwastherethemaster@gmail.com